VENI, VIDI, VICI

VENI, VIDI, VICI

*Conquer Your Enemies,
Impress Your Friends with
Everyday Latin*

EUGENE EHRLICH

A Hudson Group Book

HarperPerennial
A Division of HarperCollinsPublishers

HarperCollins books may be purchased for educational, business, or sales promotional use. For information, please write: Special Markets Department, HarperCollins Publishers, Inc., 10 East 53rd Street, New York, NY 10022.

Designed by Alma Orenstein

Library of Congress Cataloging-in-Publication Data

Ehrlich, Eugene H.
    Veni vidi vici : conquer your enemies, impress your friends with everyday Latin / Eugene Ehrlich.
        p.   cm.
    "A Hudson Group book."
    Includes index.
    ISBN 0-06-273365-6
    1. English language—Foreign words and phrases—Latin—Dictionaries. 2. Proverbs, Latin—Translations into English.
3. Maxims, Latin—Translations into English. 4. Latin language—Terms and phrases. I. Title.
PE1582.L3E38 1995
422'.471—dc20   94-42354

96 97 98 99 ❖/RRD 10 9 8 7 6 5 4

To Sam, Mickey, Hazel, Rebecca, Margie, Alice, Harry and Ruth

veni   I came
vidi   I saw
vici   I conquered

. . .

—the best-known Latin sentence of them all, freely rendered as "a piece of cake," reported by Plutarch to have been uttered by Julius Caesar by way of reporting his victory in 47 B.C. over Pharnaces, king of Pontus.

Contents

Acknowledgments

I wish particularly to thank my wife, Norma Ehrlich, for her unstinting support over the years and for her excellent assistance in interpreting many of the Latin phrases presented in this volume. Her fresh eye and keen insight helped me keep serious problems down to a minimum.

Carol Cohen at HarperCollins, as usual over our many years of association, showed enthusiasm for this book right from the start and, with genuine and unsparing assistance from Erica Spaberg, saw the book through to completion.

Finally, I wish to express my admiration and gratitude to William F. Buckley, Jr., that vigorous stylist and promoter of good diction, for his introduction to *Amo, Amas, Amat and More*, which caught the eye of so many readers.

Preface

Amo, Amas, Amat and More, the predecessor of *Veni, Vidi, Vici*, has remained in print both at home and abroad since it was first published by HarperCollins in 1985. Since that time, my interest in collecting interesting and useful Latin expressions has not flagged. Some of the words and phrases I've collected were provided by readers of *Amo, Amas, Amat and More*, others by my continuing reading of authors who write in English but express themselves in Latin from time to time. My files of Latin expressions finally reached a critical mass over a year ago, and the present volume began to take form. It is my hope that *Veni, Vidi, Vici* will prove at least as entertaining and instructive for readers—judging by letters I have received—as *Amo, Amas, Amat and More*.

In the present volume the reader will find only a few of the entries that appeared in *Amo, Amas, Amat and More* but in every case such phrases are subsumed under new entries to which they are related in meaning. Thus, whenever a reader wonders why I have not included phrases known to that reader, one explanation is that I did not want to repeat wholesale the entry list of *Amo, Amas, Amat and More*. Of course, another explanation is that I have been remiss in *Veni, Vidi, Vici*.

As in the previous volume, the attempt is made in many entries of this book to supply enlightening free translations as well as literal translations. Again as in the previous volume, most of the entries in this book date back to classical times, but there is some treatment of phrases that came into use long after the decline of the Roman Empire. It will be seen that this book presents a greater proportion of maxims and proverbs than are found in its predecessor, but the criteria for inclusion remain the same—the inherent wisdom reflected in the thought presented and the insight the entries provide into a civilization that still captures modern imagination.

Now to repeat a few words from *Amo, Amas, Amat and More* about the pronunciations supplied in this book. No one knows just how Latin was pronounced by the Romans. I was taught by my instructors at Townsend Harris High School and the City College of New York to pronounce the name *Caesar* as though the first letter were a *k.* Others may pronounce that first letter as though it were *ch*, as in *chew*. This difference, along with several other questions of pronunciation, is moot. Let me assure the reader, however, that using the pronunciations offered in this book will make it possible to pronounce Latin without incurring the scorn of most people who have studied the language in American public schools.

EUGENE EHRLICH

Pronunciation Notes

This volume uses a respelling scheme to represent the sounds of Latin. Stresses are indicated by typographic means.

Stress. Stressed syllables are shown in capital letters, and unstressed syllables as well as words of a single syllable are shown in lower case. Thus *Deo* (to God) is pronounced DAY-oh, *virtus* (virtue) is pronounced WIHR-tuus, and *ars* (art) is pronounced ahrs.

Vowels. Like English vowels, certain Latin vowels have various qualities. The samples given here help in sounding out the Latin words in the pages that follow.

Pronunciation		English	Latin Word	Latin Pronunciation
AH *or* ah	*as in*	far	*fabula*	FAH-buu-lah
AY *or* ay	*as in*	fake	*fecere*	FAY-keh-reh
AW *or* aw	*as in*	tall	*hominem*	HAW-mih-nem
E *or* e	*as in*	pet	*et*	et
EH *or* eh	*as in*	pet	*petere*	PEH-teh-reh
EE *or* ee	*as in*	sweet	*vita*	WEE-tah
IH *or* ih	*as in*	dig	*signum*	SIH-gnuum
OH *or* oh	*as in*	both	*dolor*	DOH-lawr
OO *or* oo	*as in*	moon	*unum*	OO-nuum
UU *or* uu	*as in*	put	*unum*	OO-nuum

After the letter *q*, and sometimes after *g* and *s*, the Latin *u* has the sound made by the English *w*. This is no surprise for speakers of English. Consider the words *quick*, *guava*, and *suave*. Thus, *quandoque* (sometimes) is pronounced kwahn-DOH-kweh.

Diphthongs. Like English, in which, for example, the diphthong *oi* is given a single sound (as in *point*) and *ou* is given a single sound (as in *loud*), Latin has its share of diphthongs.

Diphthong	Pronunciation	English		Latin Word	Latin Pronunciation
ae	Ī	*as in*	my	*Caesar*	KĪ-sahr
ae	ī	*as in*	my	*lacrimae*	LAH-krih-mī
au	OW or ow	*as in*	now	*Augustus*	ow-GUU-stuus
ei	AY or ay	*as in*	faint	*deinde*	DAYN-deh
eu	HEHOO	(no equivalent)		*eheu*	eh-HEHOO*
oe	OY or oy	*as in*	boy	*proelium*	PROY-lee-uum
ui	OOEE or ooee	*as in*	phooey	*huius*	HOOEE-uus

*Pronounce as a single sound: HEHOO as a blend of HEH and OO, not pronouncing the second H.

Consonants. Latin consonants are pronounced in the same way as their English equivalents, with the following exceptions.

1. The Latin *c* is pronounced as though it were a *k*. Thus *Cicero* is pronounced KIH-keh-roh.
2. The Latin *g* is always pronounced like the *g* in the English word *give*. Thus, *geometria* (geometry) is pronounced gay-oh-MEH-tree-ah, and *dignus* (worthy) is pronounced DIH-gnuus.
3. The Latin *s* is always pronounced like the *s* in the English word *set* or *pest* or *pets*. Thus, *semper paratus* (always ready) is pronounced SEM-pehr pah-RAH-tuus.
4. A *j* is often seen before a vowel in some Latin texts where one would expect to see an *i*. Whichever letter is used, the sound is taken as an initial *y*, as in the English word *young*. This means that the *i* (as well as the *j*) functions as a consonant. Thus, the Latin word for *law*, whether spelled *ius* or *jus*, is pronounced yoos, but when *i* appears before a consonant, *i* is pronounced as a vowel. As speakers of a modern language, we are not dismayed by such apparent anomalies. Consider the pronunciation of the English word *union* (initial syllable

YOON) and that of the English word *unable* (initial syllable un).

5. The Latin *v* is always pronounced as though it were a *w*. Thus, *veni, vidi, vici* is pronounced WAY-nee, WEE-dee, WEE-kee; and *ave atque vale* (hail and farewell) is pronounced AH-weh AHT-kweh WAH-lay.

English pronunciation. In many entries in this volume, Latin phrases are given English pronunciations as well as Latin pronunciations. This is done for Latin phrases that have been taken into the English language and given distinctive pronunciations. Such words are respelled for the reader in readily recognizable letter combinations to show the English pronunciations.

In the case of one sound, respelling is not sufficient, so an additional symbol is needed to approximate English pronunciation. The symbol ə (schwa) is used to indicate the indistinct vowel sound represented by the first syllable of the English word *ago* (ə-GOH) and the second syllable of the English word *ever* (EV-ər). Thus, while the Latin pronunciation of *sui generis* can be given as SOO-ee GEH-neh-rihs, the English pronunciation would appear as SOO-ee JEN-ə-rəs.

Dramatis Personae

Caesar. *Gaius Iulius Caesar.* 100–44 B.C. Born at Rome. Soldier, statesman. *Bellum Gallicum* (*The Gallic War*), *Bellum civile* (*The Civil War*).

Cato. *Marcus Porcius Cato.* 234–149 B.C. Born in Tusculum, in central Italy. Roman statesman. *De agricultura* (*On Agriculture*).

Catullus. *Gaius Valerius Catullus.* 84?-54? B.C. Born at Verona, in Cisalpine Gaul. Best known for his tempestuous love affair with a Roman gentlewoman (probably the notorious Clodia), whom he immortalized in his poems under the pseudonym Lesbia. *Carmina* (*Poems*).

Cicero. *Marcus Tullius Cicero.* 106–43 B.C. Born at Arpinum in central Italy. Jurist, statesman, writer, philosopher. *Orationes* (*Orations*), *Rhetorica* (*Writings on Rhetoric*), *Philosophica* (*Political and Philosophical Writings*), *Epistulae* (*Letters*).

Claudian. *Claudius Claudianus.* A.D. 4th cent.–c. 404. From Alexandria. A speaker of Greek. Came to Italy and mastered Latin, which was the language of his writings. Court poet under the emperor Honorius; his poetry eulogized his patrons. *De consulatu Honorii* (*On the Consulship of Honorius*), *De consolatu Stilichonis* (*On the Consulship of Stilicho*).

Epicurus. 341–270 B.C. Born at Samos, a Greek island in the Aegean. Moral and natural philosopher. Our knowledge of his system derives to a great extent from the Roman poet Lucretius. *Epistulae* (*Letters*), Κύριαι Δοξαι (*Kyriai Doxai, Principal Doctrines*).

Horace. *Quintus Horatius Flaccus.* 65–8 B.C. Born at Venusia, in southern Italy. Member of the literary circle brought together by Maecenas under the patronage of the emperor Augustus. *Carmina (Odes), Epodi (Epodes), Satirae (Satires), Epistulae (Verse Letters), Ars Poetica (The Poetic Art).*

Juvenal. *Decimus Iunius Iuvenalis.* A.D. 1st–2nd cent. Born at Aquinum, Italy. Author of verse satires attacking corruption of Roman society. *Satirae (Satires).*

Livy. *Titus Livius.* 59 B.C.–A.D. 17 or 64 B.C.–A.D. 12. Born at Padua, in northeastern Italy. Historian. *Ab urbe condita* ([History of Rome] *from the Founding of the City).*

Lucan. *Marcus Annaeus Lucanus.* A.D. 39–65. Born at Cordoba, in Spain. Courtier in the reign of Nero. Fell from grace and eventually was forced to commit suicide after becoming implicated in the Pisonian conspiracy. *Pharsalia.*

Lucretius. *Titus Lucretius Carus.* Prob. 94–55 B.C. Probably member of an aristocratic family, the Lucretii. Poet and philosopher. *De rerum natura (On the Nature of the Universe).*

Manilius. *Marcus Manilius.* 1st cent B.C.–A.D. 1st cent. Facts of his life unknown. *Astronomica* (a didactic poem on astrology).

Marcus Aurelius. *Marcus Aurelius Antoninus.* A.D. 121–180. Roman emperor. *Meditationes (Meditations).*

Martial. *Marcus Valerius Martialus.* c. A.D. 40–c. 104. Born at Bilbilis, in Spain. Depicted Roman society in epigrammatic verse. *Epigrammata (Epigrams).*

Ovid. *Publius Ovidius Naso.* 43 B.C.–A.D. 17. Born at Sulmo, in central Italy. Intended by his father for a legal career, but gave it up to devote himself to poetry. Member of the literary circle of Messalla. Exiled to an island in the Black Sea by Augustus, who was offended by Ovid's *Ars Amatoria,* though there may have been other offenses as well. *Amores (Love Poems), Ars Amatoria (The Amatory Art), Metamorphoses.*

Persius. *Aulus Persius Flaccus.* A.D. 34–62. Born at Volaterrae, in northern Italy. Stoic satirist. *Satirae (Satires).*

Petronius. *Petronius Arbiter*. A.D. 1st cent. Probably the courtier referred to by Tacitus as Nero's *arbiter elegantiae* (authority in matters of taste). *Satyricon*.

Phaedrus. c. 15 B.C.–c. A.D. 50. A Thracian, born a slave. Eventually became freedman in the household of the emperor Augustus. *Fabulae* (*Fables*).

Plautus. *Titus Maccius Plautus*. 3rd–2nd cent. B.C. Born at Sarsina, in central Italy. Author of comic dramas based on Greek originals.

Pliny the Elder. *Gaius Plinius*. A.D. 23/4–79. Born at Comum, now Como, in north central Italy. Military commander in Germany, provincial administrator, counselor to emperors Vespasian and Titus. *Naturalis historia* (*Natural History*).

Pliny the Younger. *Gaius Plinius Caecilius Secundus*. c. A.D. 66–c. 112. Nephew and adopted son of Pliny the Elder. Senatorial career; lawyer, civil administrator. *Epistulae* (*Letters*).

Plutarch. *L.* (?) *Mestrius Plutarchus*. Before A.D. 50–after 120. Born and lived most of his life in Chaeronea, in northeastern Greece. Prolific (over 200 titles attributed to him) and influential. *Moralia, Vitae* (*Lives*).

Publilius Syrus. 1st cent. B.C. Came to Rome as a slave, perhaps from Antioch. Author of mimes. *Sententiae* (*Maxims*).

Quintilian. *Marcus Fabius Quintilianus*. c. A.D. 30–before 100. Born at Calagurris, in Spain. Teacher of rhetoric; among his pupils was Pliny the Younger. *Institutio oratoria* (*The Teaching of Oratory*).

Seneca the Elder. *Lucius Annaeus Seneca*. c. 55 B.C.–between A.D. 37 and 41. Born at Cordoba, in Spain. Student and writer on rhetoric. *Controversiae, Suasoriae*.

Seneca the Younger. *Lucius Annaeus Seneca*. Between 4 and 1 B.C.–A.D. 65. Born at Cordoba, in Spain. Son of Seneca the Elder, counselor to Nero, philosopher, poet. *Dialogi* (*Dialogues*), *Naturales quaestiones* (*Natural Questions,* inquiries in physical science), *Apocolocyntosis* (*The Pumpkinification* [of the emperor Claudius]), *Tragedies, Epigrams*.

Suetonius. *Gaius Suetonius Tranquillus*. c. A.D. 69–? Practiced law briefly, held various posts in the imperial service, secretary to the emperor Hadrian. *De vita Caesarum* (*Lives of the Caesars* [from Julius to Domitian]).

Tacitus. *Cornelius Tacitus.* c. 56 A.D.–after 115. Probably from northern Italy or Gaul. Historian, held several official posts. *Annales* (*Annals*), *Historiae* (*Histories*), *Agricola* ([biography of his father-in-law, Cnaius Iulius] *Agricola*), *Germania.*

Terence. *Publius Terentius Afer.* c. 190–159 B.C. Born in North Africa, brought to Rome as a slave. Author of comic dramas adapted from Greek models by Apollodorus of Carystus and Menander. *Andria* (*The Girl from Andros*), *Hecyra* (*The Mother-in-Law*), *Heauton timorumenos* (*The Self-Punisher*), *Eunuchus* (*The Eunuch*), *Phormio, Adelphi* (*The Brothers*).

Tertullian. *Quintus Septimius Florens Tertullianus.* c. A.D. 160–c. 240. Born at Carthage, in North Africa. Trained as a lawyer. Converted to Christianity at age 35, wrote in defense of his new faith, and on moral, ethical, and religious problems.

Varro. *Marcus Terentius Varro.* 116–27 B.C. Born at Reate, in central Italy. Wrote on language, education, history, biography, philosophy, music, medicine, architecture, literary history and philology. *De lingua latina* (*On the Latin Language*).

Vegetius. *Flavius Vegetius Renatus.* A.D. 4th–5th cent. Bureaucrat in the imperial service. *Epitome rei militaris* (*Manual of Military Affairs*).

Virgil. *Publius Vergilius Maro.* 70–19 B.C. Born near Mantua, in northeastern Italy. Early in his career deeply influenced by Catullus, member of the literary circle of Asinius Pollio. Later, through Maecenas, came under the patronage of the emperor Augustus. *Aeneid, Georgics, Eclogues.*

VENI, VIDI, VICI

A

a baculo
ah BAH-kuu-loh
with a big stick

Literally "by means of the rod." The phrase *a baculo* characterizes a threat of force—the big stick—rather than a resort to logic or to sweet talk—the carrot. *Baculum* (BAH-kuu-luum) is a stick or stave, quite useful as a convincer in hand-to-hand encounters, for example, with a night prowler. In international disputes, *baculum* might be a modern fighter-bomber.

ab agendo
ahb ah-GEN-doh
out of action

For those who prefer more formal language, *ab agendo* can also be translated as "incapacitated." But this phrase can also be taken to mean "retired"—for the extraordinarily literate, "superannuated." A final meaning is "obsolete." Thus, typewriters and typists now may be considered *ab agendo* no matter which translation you use.

ab ante
ahb AHN-teh
in advance

Literally "from before." An apt phrase for those with closed minds: "I didn't have to think. My mind was made up *ab ante*, indeed, even before the debate over the movie began."

ab antiquo
ahb ahn-TEE-kwoh
from olden times

A phrase, literally "from ancient times," useful for those who are given incurably to looking back to the good old days when. . . . "Will it ever be possible to recapture the civility shown in people's manners *ab antiquo?*"

abest
AHB-est
not present

A term useful in a roll call, literally "he (or she) is absent."

abeunt studia in mores
AH-beh-uunt STOO-dee-ah in MOH-rehs
zeal develops into habit

In this maxim from Ovid, "studies (or literary efforts) develop into habits," we are assured that hours of earnest application to what we think is good for the young will one day pay off for them. And what is good for the young is also good for the rest of us. So we all find out—perhaps later rather than sooner—that true education comprises much more than mastery of finite agglomerations of dry-as-dust facts and sterile theory.

ab hoc et ab hac et ab illa
ahb hohk et ahb hahk et ahb IL-lah
the talk of gossips

This intriguing phrase, literally "from this man, this woman, and that woman," characterizes something heard or said in general gossip, with no indication of its precise source. But the phrase, which can also be translated as "from here, there, and everywhere," may be taken as the equivalent of "indiscriminately" or "confusedly." When the phrase is uttered by a clever child (who has some Latin), it offers a splendid way to evade a direct answer to a pesky question posed by a stern parent: "Where did you ever get such an idea?" "*Ab hoc et ab hac et ab illa.*" Obfuscatory enough for you?

ab igne ignem
ahb IH-gneh IH-gnem
as you sow, so shall you reap

Literally "from fire, fire," suggesting that we can expect to get out of something no more and no less than what we put into it. So if we sow dissension, how can we expect to reap anything but further dissension? (See also TIBI SERIS, TIBI METIS and UT SEMENTEM FECERIS, ITA METIS.)

abi in pace
AH-bih in PAH-keh
ciao

Literally "depart in peace," a Latin variant of **vade** (WAH-deh) **in pace**, "go in peace"—both meaning "goodbye."

abiit ad maiores (or majores)
AH-bih-eet ahd mah-YAWR-ays
he's kicked the bucket

When someone has died, we are accustomed to hearing such euphemisms as "she has passed away" and "he was laid to rest." The Romans did not do much better in *abiit ad maiores,* "he (or she) has gone to the ancestors." And if more than one person has achieved this state, the correct phrase is *abierunt* (ah-bih-EH-ruunt, "they have gone") *ad maiores.*

abiit, excessit, evasit, erupit
AH-bih-eet eks-KAYS-sit eh-WAH-sit eh-ROO-pit
he's flown the coop

There's no doubt about what is being said—"he has gone, he has made off, he has escaped, he has broken away." And who is he? Catiline, the profligate Roman noble who conspired in 63 B.C. to overthrow the government of Rome. And who is saying this? Cicero, the Roman statesman and orator, flaunting his eloquence in this sentence of his second oration against Catiline. (For additional information on Catiline's career, see ALIENI APPETENS.)

ab inconvenienti
ahb in-kawn-wen-ee-EN-tee
from inconvenience

A rhetorical term characterizing an argument—a proof—designed to show that the opposite point of view is untenable because of the inconvenience or hardship it would create. The full phrase designating such a proof is *argumentum* (ahr-goo-MEN-tuum) *ab inconvenienti*.

ab integro
ahb IN-teh-groh
anew *or* afresh

This phrase suggests a new beginning. We can all hear an earnest father or son (with some Latin, of course) saying, "Let's start *ab integro* if we can and see whether we can make a go of it once more."

abnormis sapiens crassaque Minerva
ahb-NOHR-mihs SAH-pih-ayns KRAHS-sah-kweh mih-NEHR-wah
a natural-born philosopher with nothing but horse sense

Horace, in his *Satires*, characterizing someone, literally "an unorthodox sage of rough genius," with valuable insights to offer despite—because of?—a lack of academic training. Horace tells us that this person is uninspired by Minerva, the Roman goddess of wisdom.

absens heres non erit
AHB-sens HAY-rays nohn EHR-it
absence doesn't make the heart grow fonder

This realistic maxim, "the absent one will not be the heir," cautions against complacency. Anyone who thinks an expected inheritance is in the bag may not pay sufficient attention to a wealthy family member before it is too late to do so. More broadly, it warns the unwary that there's many a slip between cup and lip—a promised political plum may not prove to be a sure thing, and having the inside track for a lucrative contract does not mean one can rest easy until the contract is signed. Intimate knowledge of *absens heres non erit* is what keeps hordes of lobbyists on the job, haunting the halls of Congress especially when an important piece of legislation is being written. Remember that it ain't over till the fat lady sings.

absente reo
ahb-SEN-teh RAY-oh
you have to show up

A legal term, "the defendant being absent," suggesting that failure of a defendant to appear in court when summoned can scarcely be considered an indication of innocence.

absolvi meam animam
ahb-SAWL-wee MAY-ahm AHN-ih-mahm
there, I got that off my chest

Once you have confessed your peccadillo or even something worse, you may be impelled to say or think *absolvi meam animam*, literally "I have set my mind free." (See also LIBERAVI ANIMAM MEAM.)

absque argento omnia vana
AHB-skweh ahr-GEN-toh AWM-nee-ah WAH-nah
first you must put food on the table

Who will contest this aphorism, literally "without money all efforts are useless"? Not George Bernard Shaw, who went much further: "Lack of money is the root of all evil." And what about Paul, in *Timothy*: "Love of money is the root of all evil"? Could they both have been right?

absque hoc
AHB-skweh hohk
without this

A legal term used in a formal denial of an allegation. "You have produced no witness to the crime, and *absque hoc* there is no basis for holding my client responsible."

absque ulla conditione
AHB-skweh UUL-lah kawn-dih-tih-OHN-eh
no ifs, ands, or buts

Literally "without any condition." When one surrenders *absque ulla conditione*—whether to a superior military force or to the strength of authority or to moral suasion—nothing is to be held back. "You will have that report on my desk at close of business today, *absque ulla conditione*." No excuses will be tolerated, no conditions, no reservations. And that's the way the real world works.

abundans cautela non nocet
ah-BUUN-dahns KOW-teh-lah nohn NAW-ket
you can't be too careful

Literally "abundant caution does no harm." In general, being told to look before you leap is good advice, but if we look too many times before we leap, we may find that a golden opportunity has passed us by.

abundant dulcibus vitiis
ah-BUUN-dahnt DUUL-kih-buus WIH-tih-ees
nobody's perfect

An indulgent characterization, literally "they abound with lovely faults," from Quintilian, who knew and enjoyed an engaging foible when he encountered one. (See also VITIIS NEMO SINE NASCITUR.)

ab universali ad particulare valet, a particulari ad universale non valet consequentia

ahb OO-nih-wehr-SAH-lih ahd pahr-tih-koo-LAH-reh WAH-let ah pahr-tih-koo-LAH-rih ahd oo-nih-wehr-SAH-leh nohn WAH-let kawn-seh-KWEN-tih-ah

let's get our logic straight

We reason logically when we apply a general truth—but let's be sure the general truth is universally correct—about a group to individual members of that group: *ab universali ad particulare valet,* "inference from the universal to the particular is valid." The valid syllogism we all wrestled with in our college days put it this way: "All A is C, all B is A, therefore all B is C." Dangerous stereotyping can result from the logical error of reasoning from the particular to the general: *a particulari ad universale non valet consequentia,* "inference from the particular to the universal is not valid." Too frequently encountered today are a great number of outrageous attitudes that can be represented as a faulty syllogism: "He's a member of X group, he is a terrible person, therefore all members of X group are terrible persons." Watch out.

a caelo usque ad centrum

ah KĪ-loh UUS-kweh ahd KEN-truum

property rights

A phrase in real estate deeds defining the extent of a landowner's holdings, literally "from heaven to the center." That is, while a deed will surely spell out the length and breadth of the property, what about the space above it and the land beneath it? What part of these does the landowner own? The answer is quite clear, *a caelo usque ad centrum,* everything above the land and everything below it—all the way to the center of the earth. Today we may speak of "air rights" and "mineral rights." A pale imitation of "from heaven to the center of the earth."

acceptissima semper munera sunt auctor quae pretiosa facit
ahk-kep-TEES-sih-mah SEM-pehr MOO-neh-rah suunt OWK-tawr kwī preh-tee-OH-sah FAH-keet
it's the thought behind a gift that counts

An aphorism from Ovid, more literally "most acceptable always are the gifts that the giver makes precious." Now get out there and find something inexpensive and memorable for the newly married couple. Wal-mart anyone?

accusare nemo se debet, nisi coram deo
ahk-koo-SAH-reh NAY-moh say DAY-bet NIH-sih KOH-rahm DAY-oh
taking the Fifth

A phrase in law, "no one is bound to accuse himself (or herself) unless before God." This is one of the human rights spelled out in the U.S. Bill of Rights, Article V of which includes the words "nor shall be compelled in any criminal case to be a witness against himself." Article V is generally known as the Fifth Amendment, and the process of invoking the Fifth Amendment to refuse to answer possibly self-incriminating questions before a grand jury, in court testimony, or in other sworn official interrogations is known informally as "taking the Fifth." In the phrase *nisi coram deo*, "unless before God," the full Latin formulation does not rule out the possibility of answering fully to higher authority.

acerrima proximorum odia
ah-KEHR-rih-mah praw-ksih-MAW-ruum AWD-ee-ah
when families fall out

Tacitus observed in *acerrima proximorum odia* that "the bitterest hatreds are those of next of kin," which was also true in Biblical times—recall, for example, the brothers Cain and

Abel—and is still true today. For a modern example, consider the Thanksgiving and Christmas feasts in some families that end in bitter arguments stemming from remembered past slights and smoldering enmities among those present. Again, in some parts of our culture, the joy of weddings too often gives way to disputes—even to fisticuffs and lethal violence— among the wedding guests. We take comfort in knowing that such behavior was not uncommon in Roman times. (See also AD INTERNECIONEM.)

ac etiam
ahk EH-tee-ahm
and also *or* and even

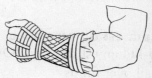

acti labores iucundi (or jucundi)
AH-ktih lah-BOH-rays yoo-KUUN-dee
satisfaction in a job well done

The phrase *acti labores iucundi*, "labors accomplished are pleasant," recognizes that for a small number of fortunate people among us, work itself can bring great satisfaction, even joy. And when these productive people achieve something gratifying, they are eager to get on to the next task. No TGIF—thank God it's Friday—for them.

actio personalis moritur cum persona
AH-ktee-oh pehr-soh-NAH-lihs MAW-rih-tuur kuum pehr-SOH-nah
dead men don't sue

A legal principle, "a personal action dies with the person," stemming from common law, the unwritten law based on custom or earlier court decisions. Thus—in certain courts, at least—a personal suit undertaken against another is voided when the plaintiff dies.

actum agere
AH-ktuum AH-geh-reh
this looks familiar

A double-barreled characterization, "to do what has already been done," with two implicit meanings. 1. Cease your endless tinkering with work you have already completed; you'll surely ruin it. 2. Avoid plagiarism—even of your own work. (See also ACTUM NE AGAS.)

actum est de republica
AH-ktuum est day ray-POO-blih-kah
it's all over for us

Many among us, alarmists by nature, are quick to give up on society when things appear to be going badly. Thus, faced with a few signs of deterioration in our government, we may immediately pronounce the entire nation in imminent danger of collapse and take to the airwaves with eloquent, albeit premature, obsequies. Of course, our Chicken Littles sometimes prove correct—the sky is indeed falling. Such was the case with the once-powerful Roman empire, when the statement *actum est de republica*, literally "it's all over with the commonwealth," proved to be true. When we contemplate making alarming pronouncements, it behooves us nevertheless to think twice before unduly alarming the unwary. Maybe, after all, the sky is not really falling. (But maybe it is.)

actum ne agas
AH-ktuum nay AH-gahs
let well enough alone

This advice from Terence, "don't do yet again what is already done," counsels against tampering with a completed work. Anyone who continually tinkers in this way will never get done—and usually won't actually improve the work. Writers: When you feel like going back over your words for the umpteenth time, turn on your printer and call Federal Express to pick up the printout. Or just send off a floppy disk or two. (See also ACTUM AGERE.)

actus dei nemini facit iniuriam (or injuriam)
AH-ktuus DAY-ee NAY-mih-nih FAHK-eet in-YOO-ree-ahm
sorry, we have to reject your claim

This is the "act of God" principle, literally "an act of God injures nobody," which gets insurance companies off the hook when property or lives are damaged, for example, by abnormal tides, earthquakes, lightning, or storms. The idea is that such natural phenomena are beyond the control of ordinary mortals and so are not covered by insurance. Please look carefully at the fine print the next time you consider taking out a policy.

actus me invito factus non est meus actus
AH-ktuus may in-WEE-toh FAHK-tuus nohn est MAY-uus AH-ktuus
I was only following orders

A legal phrase, literally "an act done against my will is not my act," that makes life difficult for police officers and prosecuting attorneys. In conformity with this principle, if a person is coerced into signing an agreement, committing a crime, or confessing guilt, the law does not hold the person responsible.

actus non facit reum nisi mens est rea
AH-ktuus nohn FAH-keet RAY-uum NIH-sih mehns est RAY-ah
I never intended to kill anybody

A legal maxim, "the act does not make the accused guilty unless the mind (intention) be guilty." Those of us who are addicted to watching TV cop shows are familiar with this basis for plea bargaining: "I didn't want to hurt anyone, so you'll never prove murder one or murder two. How about manslaughter?" Now we know the Latin to use when a district attorney has us sweating.

a cuspide corona
ah KUUS-pih-deh kaw-ROH-nah
the way to get ahead

Conventional wisdom has it that every young man enrolling at West Point dreams of one day becoming President of the United States. Thus, we are not surprised to see in *a cuspide corona*, literally "from the spear a crown," that in Rome successful military service surely helped in reaching the top of the republic.

ad bivium
ahd BIH-wih-uum
at the crossroads

More literally and charmingly "at a place where two ways meet."

ad crumenam
ahd kroo-MAY-nahm
the promise of a payday for someone

A phrase, literally "to the purse," used in *argumentum* (ahr-goo-MEN-tuum) *ad crumenam*, "an appeal based on the possibility of profit." This is an almost surefire way to convince someone to go along with you in what you propose—there's profit in it for both of us. *Argumentum ad crumenam* makes for success in negotiation.

ad extremum
ahd ek-STRAY-muum
at last

The noun *extremum* may also be translated as "the extreme," and in the phrase *ad extremum virium* (WEE-rih-uum, "of powers") gives us "to the utmost of one's powers." Thus, if we wish to encourage someone to go all out in pursuing a goal, we can say, "Never give up. Work *ad extremum virium.*"

ad fidelis
ahd fih-DAY-lihs
to the faithful

When we are addressing an audience of those who need no converting to our cause, we are speaking *ad fidelis*. The phrase is employed as well to characterize a doctrine or communication meant only for believers in a specified creed, or members of a political party or church.

ad finem
ahd FEE-nem
to the end

This phrase can also be translated as "at the end" and "finally," as in "I wish *ad finem* to express my gratitude for your patience in hearing me through." In the phrase *ad finem fidelis* (fih-DAY-lihs), we have "faithful to the end." And what more can one ask of a friend or spouse?

adhibenda est in iocando (or jocando) moderatio
ahd-hih-BEN-dah est in yoh-KAHN-doh maw-deh-RAH-tee-oh
try not to offend people with your jokes

In suggesting that people keep their jokes within the bounds of good taste, literally "one should employ restraint in his jests," Cicero offered advice that many of today's politicians, newspaper columnists, after-dinner speakers, and TV and movie comedians would do well to take to heart.

a dicto secundum quid ad dictum simpliciter
ah DEE-ktoh seh-KUUN-duum kwid ahd DEE-ktuum sim-PLEE-kih-tehr
from a particular case to a general truth

This characterization criticizes the drawing of broad generalizations from a single valid observation. So when a person raised in poverty becomes a criminal, we must not fall into the trap of inferring that all persons raised in poverty will surely become criminals. (See also AB UNIVERSALI AD PARTICULARE VALET, A PARTICULARI AD UNIVERSALE NON VALET CONSEQUENTIA.)

a dicto simpliciter ad dictum secundum quid
ah DEE-ktoh sim-PLEE-kih-tehr ahd DEE-ktuum seh-KUUN-duum kwid

from a general truth to a particular case

This inversion of the preceding observation points out that we may not properly apply a generalization to a particular case without considering the possible uniqueness of that case. Even if most child-beaters were once the victims of child-beaters, we should not infer that any person who suffered this kind of treatment in childhood will surely follow the same dreadful practice as an adult.

ad ignorantiam
ahd ih-gnoh-RAHN-tee-ahm

to ignorance

In law, an argument in a trial may be based *ad ignorantiam,* that is, on one's opponent's ignorance of the facts in the case. Again, a judicial decision may be appealed *ad ignorantiam,* that is, on the basis that the case was decided without knowledge of important information that was known but went unrevealed during the trial.

ad impossibile nemo tenetur
ahd ihm-paws-SEE-bih-leh NAY-moh teh-NAY-tuur

don't be surprised when you don't bat .400

This small wisdom, "nobody is held to the impossible," is designed to prevent heartbreak. While people should strive to do their best, they must not set their hearts on goals that are virtually impossible for them to achieve.

ad initium
ahd ih-NIH-tee-uum
to *or* at the beginning

ad instar
ahd EEN-stahr
after the fashion of

This phrase may be used to indicate a literary creation or work of art done in the style of a master. Thus, an oration may be written in the style of a great orator, as *ad instar Ciceronis* (kee-keh-ROHN-ees, "in the manner of Cicero"). But *instar* may also be translated as "likeness," giving us the phrase *ad instar omnium* (AWM-nee-uum), "in the likeness of all," suggesting a lack of individuality. So if we are striving for excellence, we ought to eschew unoriginality.

ad internecionem
ahd in-tehr-neh-kee-OH-nem
to slaughter

A bloody and completely final phrase that makes a mockery of what we are used to thinking of as civilized behavior. It characterizes warfare in which no quarter is shown to an enemy army. Thus, "a war *ad internecionem*" is a war of extermination, and the noun *internecio*, which may be translated as "massacre" or "extermination," suggests the brutality shown in modern times in the term "Holocaust" or more recently in so-called "ethnic cleansing." It is worth pointing out that the English adjective "internecine" most correctly conveys the meaning of "mutually destructive," but in "internecine strife" has taken on the meaning of "a struggle or conflict within a group." While the etymology of the term does not suggest this meaning, we must all be aware that the bitterest— even the most savage—conflicts often occur between members of a family. Consider, for example, the bloody toll of the United States Civil War, aptly characterized as a war between brothers. (See also ACERRIMA PROXIMORUM ODIA, which tells us that less than civilized behavior has been with us throughout recorded time.)

ad invidiam
ahd in-WIH-dih-ahm

to envy

This phrase is used to characterize an argument or appeal—*argumentum* (ahr-goo-MEN-tuum) *ad invidiam*—not based on reason or supporting evidence yet powerful in effect and frequently employed by the unscrupulous rabble-rouser, always ready to appeal to envy, jealousy, prejudice, malice, or ill will.

ad iudicium (or judicium)
ahd yoo-DIH-kee-uum

to common sense

This phrase, literally "to judgment," is used to characterize an argument or appeal, *argumentum* (ahr-goo-MEN-tuum) *ad iudicium*, based on logic or factual evidence, which can be counted on to convince reasonable people. Or can it?

adiuvante (or adjuvante) Deo labor proficit
ahd-yuu-WAHN-teh DAY-oh LAH-bawr PRAW-fih-kit

with God's help, work prospers

A humble response to such intrusive questions as "How's business?" and "How's the novel coming?"

ad manum
ahd MAH-nuum

in readiness

A happy phrase, literally "at hand," telling the world, for example, that an assignment, project, or the like is complete. But it can also be used more widely. "The money for this month's mortgage payment is *ad manum*." "She soon became aware that the solution to her problem was not *ad manum*."

ad meliora vertamur
ahd meh-lee-OH-rah WEHR-tah-muur
let's change the subject

A handy expression, literally "let us turn to better things," useful for turning attention away from an embarrassing or depressing subject that is under discussion. (See also SED HAEC HACTENUS.)

ad misericordiam
ahd mih-seh-rih-KAWR-dih-ahm
to pity

When all other arguments fail, one can appeal *ad miseri-cordiam*, hoping that a court or one's opponent will be moved to show sympathy and grant mercy—both "sympathy" and "mercy" are additional translations of *misericordia*.

ad modum
ahd MAW-duum
like

This phrase, also rendered as "after the manner of," provides an opportunity to employ the compressed Latin phrase in place of its lengthier—and more common—English equivalent: "It would not be farfetched to say the young violinist played *ad modum* Heifetz." By adding *hunc* (huunk) to *ad modum*, we get *ad hunc modum,* "like this." A useful locution: "If you carry on *ad hunc modum*, you'll gain nothing."

ad multos annos
ahd MUUL-tohs AHN-nohs
l'chaim

A toast, of course, literally "for many years," and often taken as "long life!" although "to life," as given above in Hebrew, will also do. The more common Latin toast is **prosit** (PROH-sit), "may it benefit you," but it is also translated as any of the three English renderings here given.

ad oculos
ahd AW-kuu-lohs
visibly

> Literally "to the eyes."

adscriptus glebae
ahd-SKREE-ptuus GLAY-bī
attached to the soil

This phrase is not intended to characterize an avid week-end gardener, much less a farmer. Rather it applies to a serf and surely indicates the absence of personal freedom. A serf was attached to the soil in the sense of being in a condition of servitude to the lord he served, but in addition, along with the land the serf worked, the serf was transferrable from one owner to the next. Incidentally, while *gleba* (GLAY-bah) may be translated as "soil," it also may be taken as "a clod of earth," making *adscriptus glebae* an especially ugly phrase describing a slave.

ad summam
ahd SUUM-mahm
in short

Also translated as "in fact," "in a word," and "in conclusion," *ad summam* is useful especially when the words following it are brief and to the point. *Summam* is a form of the noun *summa* (SUUM-mah), meaning "chief point" and "summary" and other similar terms. *Ad summam* must not be confused with the following entry, AD SUMMUM, employing a form of *summus* (SUUM-muus), meaning "highest."

ad summum
ahd SUUM-muum
to the highest point

Also taken as "to the surface" and "to the top," and the phrase *summum bonum* (SUUM-muum BAW-nuum) means "the highest good." All speakers of English will see the noun "summit" lurking in the adjective *summus* (SUUM-muus), "highest." (See the previous entry, AD SUMMAM, for a useful clarification.)

ad usum
ahd OOS-uum
according to custom

This phrase may also be taken as "according to usage," giving lexicographers as well as social commentators a peg on which to hang their judgmental pronouncements.

ad verecundiam
ahd weh-ray-KUUN-dih-ahm
to reverence

An argument appealing to reverence—or to modesty, a second meaning of *verecundia*—is an *argumentum* (ahr-goo-MEN-tuum) *ad verecundiam*, suggesting that logic and substantial evidence are noticeably absent from the discourse. If Samuel Johnson was correct in instructing us that "patriotism is the last refuge of a scoundrel," *argumentum ad verecundiam* appears to be a close runner-up.

adversa virtute repello
ahd-WEHR-sah wihr-TOO-teh reh-PEL-loh
I repulse adversity by courage (or valor)

Maybe so, but not when I'm confronted by an armed mugger. After all, a 16th-century proverb teaches us that discretion is the better part of valor. (See also NOLI IRRITARE LEONES.)

aegroto dum anima est spea esse dicitur
ī-GROH-toh duum AH-nih-mah est SPAY-ah ES-seh DEE-kih-tuur
where there's life, there's hope

Cicero telling us, more literally, "as long as a sick man has breath, he has hope." Too often, a slender reed to which to cling.

aemulatio vicini
ī-muu-LAH-tee-oh WEE-kih-nih
neighborly envy

In law the phrase, literally "the ill will of a neighbor," telling us that it is illegal for a landowner to act maliciously toward an adjacent landowner, for example, by intentionally depriving the neighbor's property of a water view.

aequabiliter et diligenter
ī-kwah-BIH-lih-tehr et dih-lih-GEN-tehr
impartially and conscientiously

A welcome phrase, useful in characterizing the actions of an admirable judge or arbiter. "She conducts all hearings in her court *aequabiliter et diligenter.*"

aequam memento rebus in arduis servare mentem
Ī-kwahm meh-MEN-toh RAY-buus in AHR-duu-ees sehr-WAH-reh MEN-tem
keep your cool

Horace advising us to "remember to keep an unruffled mind in difficulties." To which those of us who are weak reply, "Easier said than done." Yet Rudyard Kipling thought so highly of the advice that he put it this way in his once-beloved poem "If":

> If you can keep your head when all about you
> Are losing theirs and blaming it on you. . .

(See also SAEVIS TRANQUILLUS IN UNDIS.)

aes alienum
īs ah-lih-AYN-uum
debt

Any stockbroker should keep in mind that *aes alienum*, while meaning "debt" or "borrowed money," translates literally as "another's money." Something to keep in mind when touting a penny stock or suggesting a risky investment—especially to widows and orphans. (See AES SUUM.)

aes suum
īs SOO-uum
one's own money

Just as it is important for stockbrokers to keep AES ALIENUM (see above) in mind when recommending investments to clients, it is also suggested that the brokers keep *aes suum* in mind. Thus admonished, brokers will treat their clients' money with the same care given to the brokers' own money. A word of caution: some people acting in a fiduciary role have been known to become too literal in treating their clients' money as their own.

aeternum servans sub pectore vulnus
ī-TEHR-nuum SEHR-wahns suub PEH-ktaw-reh WUUL-nuus
bearing a grudge

The human animal has an unsurpassed ability to remember, but does that gift always work to our advantage? Not in all circumstances, according to Virgil, who characterized Juno's undying hatred for the Trojans as *aeternum servans sub pectore vulnus*, "nursing an everlasting wound within the breast." Today, of course, we are too enlightened to nurse grudges for very long.

afflatus
ahf-FLAH-tuus
inspiration

This term, also given as *adflatus* (ahd-FLAH-tuus), has as its primary meanings "breath," "breeze," and "wind," suggesting the belief of ancient Romans that a divine source breathed upon the writer or artist to impart inspiration. And "inspiration" itself derives from the Latin verb **inspirare** (in-spih-RAH-reh, "breathe upon *or* into"). For many centuries, of course, "*afflatus*" (ə-FLAY-təs) has had a place in the English language, with the meaning "inspiration."

afflavit Deus et dissipantur
ahf-FLAH-wit DAY-uus et dis-sih-PAHN-tuur
God breathed and they were put to flight

This is one version of the inscription on a medal struck in commemoration of the destruction of the Spanish Armada in 1588. The inscription is also given as *flavit Jehovah et dissipati sunt* (FLAH-wit yeh-HAW-wah et dis-sih-PAH-tee suunt), "Jehovah breathed and they were dispersed." You might think that Sir Frances Drake and the English fleet had something to do with the victory, but it is recorded that mighty storms at sea during the period of the battle were of great assistance in destroying the Spanish fleet. So there is some credence for the divine intervention suggested by both versions of the inscription on the medal. Note that neither inscription said anything about Drake or his cohorts. Whether you accept the idea of divine intervention is for you to decide.

a fonte puro pura defluit aqua
ah FAWN-teh POO-roh POO-rah deh-FLOO-it AH-kwah
from a pure spring flows pure water

A thought whose verity extends far beyond water sources. For example, it could be used to characterize the content of a sermon preached by a favorite minister, or to describe the thoughts expressed by an innocent child.

agenti incumbit probatio
ah-GEN-tee in-KUUM-bit praw-BAH-tih-oh
the burden of proof falls on the one bringing the suit

A principle established in Roman law and still followed widely today. It has the effect in a criminal trial, for example, of obliging the prosecutor to present evidence that the court or jury could reasonably believe in support of the contention that the accused person is guilty as charged, failing which the case will be lost. *Agenti incumbit probatio* defines the so-called "burden of proof," in Latin *onus probandi* (AW-nuus praw-BAHN-dee), literally "the burden of proving." In civil cases, the burden of proof falls on the attorney for the person who has made the charge and seeks redress.

alea belli incerti
AH-lay-ah BEL-lee in-KEHR-tee
you never know how a war will turn out

This insight, literally "the hazard of war is uncertain," has given rise to a profession whose function is to predict the chances of success or failure in a contemplated military venture. These analysts are employed by governments and think tanks, and we read their articles in learned journals, buy their books, and watch many of them pontificating on television news and talk shows. Whether these experts prove right, almost right, or hopelessly wrong in their analyses of a given situation does not seem to affect their professional standing; they merely move on to the next prediction, never mentioning earlier inaccuracies. Notice that Caesar's portentous remark **alea iacta est** (AH-lay-ah YAH-ktah est, commonly expressed as "the die is cast"), refers to the game of dice, which supports the notion that launching a war is always a gamble.

aliam excute quercum
AH-lee-ahm eks-KOO-teh KWEHR-kuum
get lost!

A colorful Latin phrase to use in turning down a proposition or denying a request for a favor, usually a loan. The response *aliam excute quercum*, literally "shake out some other oak," tells the person to whom it is addressed that he or she should look elsewhere.

alia tendanda via est
AH-lee-ah ten-DAHN-dah WEE-ah est
go back to the drawing board

More literally "another way must be tried," suggesting strongly that someone's present efforts will prove fruitless.

aliena optimum frui insania
ah-lee-AY-nah AW-ptih-muum FROO-ee in-SAH-nee-ah
learn from the mistakes of others

The intent of this observation, more literally "it's a very good thing to enjoy the folly of others," is to encourage us not to repeat mistakes made by other people. Too often, such advice falls on deaf ears and we are doomed to repeat past mistakes.

alienatus a se
ah-lee-eh-NAH-tuus ah say
deranged

An apt characterization of a person afflicted with a psychological disorder, literally "estranged from oneself."

aliena vitia in oculis habemus, a tergo nostra sunt
ah-lee-AY-nah WIH-tee-ah in AWK-uu-lihs hah-BAY-muus, ah TEHR-goh NAW-strah suunt

> Oh wad some power the giftie gie us
> To see oursels as others see us!

In these lines Robert Burns told us that while we are quick to recognize shortcomings of character in other people, we are blind to our own. Seneca expressed the same thought in *aliena vitia in oculis habemus, a tergo nostra sunt*, literally "another's faults are before our eyes, our own are behind us." (See also ALIQUIS NON DEBET ESSE IUDEX IN PROPRIA CAUSA.)

alieni appetens
ah-lee-AY-nee AHP-peh-tens
covetous

This phrase, literally "greedy for another's property," describes covetousness, second among the seven deadly sins and tenth among the Ten Commandments. *Alieni appetens* also is part of a larger phrase, *alieni appetens, sui profusus* (SOO-ee praw-FOO-suus). This larger phrase has the literal meaning "covetous for another's property, wasteful of his own." Sallust, a 1st-century B.C. Roman historian, used it to characterize Catiline, the Roman nobleman whose conspiratorial activities made him a target of Cicero and Cicero's supporters. Since human failings have not changed all that much since the 1st century B.C., we can still find use for *alieni appetens, sui profusus.* (See also QUOUSQUE TANDEM ABUTERE PATIENTIA NOSTRA?)

alio intuitu
AH-lee-oh in-TOO-ih-too
from another point of view

When the search for a solution to a vexing problem hits a snag, the thing to do is seek out someone with a fresh mind to review the problem *alio intuitu.* It is surprising how often such a review will quickly yield worthwhile suggestions. Incidentally, *intuitu* is a participial form of the verb *intueri* (in-too-AY-ree), "gaze at" or "contemplate." Which leads one to think that the phenomenon we call "intuition" is not as mysterious as commonly thought—a little contemplation can give us a fresh point of view.

aliquis in omnibus, nullus in singulis
AH-lih-kwihs in AWM-nih-buus NUUL-luus in SIN-guu-lees
jack-of-all-trades, master of none

A phrase, more literally "a somebody in general, a nobody in particular," used to describe a generalist rather than an expert in a given area, for example, a handyman (or handyperson) as opposed to a craftsman (or craftsperson).

aliquis non debet esse iudex (or judex) in propria causa
AH-lih-kwihs nohn DAY-bet ES-seh YOO-deks in PRAW-pree-ah KOW-sah
how can we be objective in judging ourselves?

This Latin maxim, "nobody should be a judge in his (or her) own case," makes it clear that we cannot be trusted to evaluate ourselves or our own work. Wise judges, expert editors, even qualified art or drama or music critics can be counted on for greater objectivity—within the limits of their ability, that is.

alitur vitium vivitque tegendo
AH-lih-tuur WIH-tih-uum wee-WIT-kweh tay-GEN-doh
whatever you do, don't stonewall

In this small example of wisdom—or at least common sense—"a fault is nourished and lives by being concealed," Virgil urges us not to give in to the human tendency to hide things that should—and inevitably will—become public knowledge despite our best efforts to prevent disclosure. Yet, too many times, the occupant of the Oval Office or well-intentioned presidential cronies ignore Virgil's advice and do their best to conceal information from the press and the public. Of course, despite their best efforts, a plethora of troublesome facts inevitably come to light and harm U.S. Presidents. When will they ever learn?

aliud corde premunt, aliud ore promunt
AH-lee-uud KAWR-deh PRAY-muunt AH-lee-uud OH-reh PRAW-muunt
no use trying to prevent leaks

Everyone knows that almost no one can keep a secret. *Aliud corde premunt, aliud ore promunt* doesn't explain why.

All it tells us is that people are blabbermouths, literally "one thing they conceal in the heart, they disclose another with the mouth." If this has been going on since Roman times at least, why should we be surprised when we read people's most important secrets on the front page of the morning newspaper? (See ALIUD EST CELARE, ALIUD TACERE.)

aliud est celare, aliud tacere
AH-lee-uud est keh-LAH-reh AH-lee-uud TAH-keh-reh
better to play dumb—or is it?

A warning for anyone with something to hide, "it's one thing to conceal, another to be silent." Thus, if someone feels constrained to prevent exposure of certain knowledge—for whatever reason—this admonition tells us that silence may be a better option than inventing a lie to cover up one's own guilt or the guilt of trusted allies. Neither path is that of the virtuous person, who knows better than to become involved in nefarious intrigues. In short, don't ever say or do anything you would hate to hear reported on the seven o'clock TV news. (See also ALITUR VITIUM VIVITQUE TEGENDO, which does not condone concealment.)

aliud et idem
AH-lee-uud et EE-dem
another thing and yet the same

We might say this of the latest work of second-rate playwrights, movie directors, and novelists who regularly clone their earlier efforts. This is also true of movies and TV programs. If they prove successful, they are immediately copied by others.

alium silere quod voles primus sile
AH-lee-uum sih-LAY-reh kwawd WAW-lehs PREE-muus
SIH-leh
the surefire way to keep a secret

Advice from Seneca, the poet, philosopher, and counselor to Emperor Nero, "if you want to keep something secret, first say nothing yourself." (For why you must not entrust a secret to others, see ALIUD CORDE PREMUNT, ALIUD ORE PROMUNT.)

allegans contraria non est audiendis
AH-lay-gahns kawn-TRAH-ree-ah nohn est ow-dee-EN-dihs
close your ears

Literally "he who alleges contradictory things is not to be listened to." How can you trust a person who speaks out of both sides of his mouth?

alma natura
AHL-mah nah-TOO-rah
fostering nature

Just as we enjoy giving universities the glorious appellation *alma mater* (MAH-tehr, "fostering mother"), in *alma natura* we infuse nature with its own golden glow. At the same time we overlook the ravages of time, the devastating impact of tsunamis and other violent acts of nature, and the occasional volcanic eruption. Fostering nature indeed!

alter ipse amicus
AHL-tehr IH-pseh ah-MEE-kuus
a friend is a second self

The Romans made much of friendship. (For example, see also AMICUS EST TANQUAM ALTER IDEM.)

alteri sic tibi
ahl-TEH-ree seek TIH-bih
do unto others

The opening words of the golden rule, in full: "Do unto others as you would have them do unto you."

altus mare
AHL-tuus MAH-reh
the high sea

A term in law designating the area of a sea or ocean that lies beyond the territorial waters of a country, and thus beyond the jurisdiction of that country.

amabilis insania
ah-MAH-bih-lihs een-SAH-nee-ah
lovable folly

A phrase of Ovid also translated as "lovable madness," since *insania* can also be taken as "madness" and as "poetic rapture." Enough said. (See also AMANS IRATUS MULTA MENTITUR SIBI.)

a maiori ad minus
ah mī-AW-ree ahd MIH-nuus
leading from strength

Said of a form of argument or proof, literally "from the greater to the less," that presents the most telling evidence first and then goes down the line to the least important. Arguing *a maiori ad minus* will at least make sure that in a trial one's best points are presented to a jury before any of the jurors nod off.

amans iratus multa mentitur sibi
AH-mahns ee-RAH-tuus MUUL-tah MEN-tih-tuur SIH-bih
an angry lover tells himself many lies

Publilius Syrus, who well understood human nature, telling us not to trust the judgment of a spurned lover. (See also AMABILIS INSANIA and AMARE ET SAPERE VIX DEO CONCEDITUR.)

amare et sapere vix deo conceditur
ah-MAH-reh et SAH-peh-reh wiks DAY-oh kawn-KEH-dih-tuur
crazy in love

Publilius Syrus, again demonstrating profound knowledge of human nature, gives us this maxim, "to love and be wise is scarcely granted even to a god." No wonder we say "mad about you." (See also AMABILIS INSANIA and AMANS IRATUS MULTA MENTITUR SIBI.)

amari aliquid
ah-MAH-ree AH-lih-kwid
a touch of bitterness

We can all be certain that sometime in our lives, and sooner rather than later, we will experience *amari aliquid*, literally "something bitter." Only young lovers think they are immune.

a mari usque ad mare
ah MAH-rih UUS-kweh ahd MAH-reh
from sea to sea

The motto of the Dominion of Canada, more literally "from the sea all the way to the sea." In "America the Beautiful," some of us sing of brotherhood "from sea to shining sea." In the case of Canada and the United States, of course, the seas are in fact oceans. But who can make a strong rhyme employing "from ocean to ocean"? Again, while the Romans had the word **oceanus** (oh-KAY-ah-nuus), which they borrowed from the Greek *ókeanós*, in Homer considered to be a river that surrounded the earth, they used *mare* more often to mean "ocean." Really now, who knew from real oceans back in ancient Rome or in Homer's time?

ambigendi locus
ahm-bih-GEN-dee LAW-kuus
room for doubt

amici fures tempores
ah-MEE-kee FOO-rehs TEM-paw-rehs
friends are thieves of time

As much as the Romans valued friendship, they knew it was a mistake to give oneself freely to friends when serious work was lying undone. And if they had invented telephones, they would surely have used answering machines. (See also DUM LOQUOR, HORA FUGIT.)

amici probantur rebus adversia
ah-MEE-kee praw-BAHN-tuur RAY-buus ahd-WEHR-see-ah
the friendship litmus test

Seneca, in "friends are proved by adversity," telling us how to tell true friends from fair-weather friends. (See also AMICUS CERTUS IN RE INCERTA CERNITUR.)

amicitia semper prodest
ah-mee-KIH-tih-ah SEM-pehr PROH-dest
don't forget your friends

Here's Seneca again on friendship, this time telling us that "friendship is always of benefit." (See also AMICI PROBANTUR REBUS ADVERSIA.)

amicus certus in re incerta cernitur
ah-MEE-kuus KEHR-tuus in ray een-KEHR-tah KEHR-nih-tuur
when things get iffy, you find out who your true friends are

Here is Cicero, quoting the 2nd-century B.C. Roman poet Quintus Ennius on the true test of friendship, telling us literally that "a reliable friend is discerned in an uncertain affair." We are more apt to say "a friend in need is a friend indeed," a locution with roots in the Latin *amicus certus in re incerta cernitur*. (For Seneca's version of this thought, see AMICI PROBANTUR REBUS ADVERSIA.)

amicus est tanquam alter idem
ah-MEE-kuus est TAHN-kwahm AHL-tehr EE-dem
a friend is just like a second self

For us such a claim applies only to a close friend, but the Romans didn't throw the term *amicus* around. For them, every friend was a close friend. (See also ALTER IPSE AMICUS.)

amissum quod nescitur non amittitur
ah-MIHS-suum kwawd NES-kih-tuur nohn ah-MIT-tih-tuur
what you don't know won't hurt you

This maxim of Publilius Syrus, "a loss that is unknown is no loss at all," offers a valuable insight that can be applied to a variety of life's travails.

amor gignit amorem
AH-mawr GIH-gnit ah-MOH-rem
love begets love

So they say. At least it's worth trying. (See also SI VIS AMARI AMA.)

amor habendi
AH-mawr hah-BEN-dee
love of possessing

A dangerous proclivity, more vividly identified by Ovid as *amor sceleratus* (skeh-leh-RAH-tuus, "accursed") *habendi*, giving us "the accursed love of possessing." Ovid clearly was thinking of the many people who carry possessing to an extreme.

amor tussique non celantur
AH-mawr TOOS-sih-kweh nohn keh-LAHN-tuur
love and a cough cannot be hidden

See also NEC AMOR NEC TUSSIS CELATUR.

aniles fabulae
ah-NEE-lehs FAH-boo-lī
old wives' tales

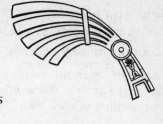

animal disputans
AHN-ih-mahl DIHS-poo-tahns
an ornery critter

An apt characterization of a curmudgeon, literally "a disputatious creature," who automatically takes exception to anything said in his presence, who casts doubt on the efficacy of every proposed idea, and who hates every new play or novel—whether or not it is one he has seen or read—thus endearing himself to one and all.

animal rationale
AHN-ih-mahl rah-tee-oh-NAH-leh
the human animal

In this self-adulatory term, literally "the reasoning animal," we humans proudly call attention to our ability to reason, which is said to differentiate us from so-called lower animals. Of course, we periodically go to war with the intention of destroying as many other people as we can and continually do our best to thoroughly foul our nests—lately with deadly chemical and nuclear waste—proving beyond any doubt that we indeed are reasoning animals.

animo et fide
AHN-ih-moh et FIH-day
by courage and faith

A motto positing that with courage and faith a family or other form of social organization will inevitably manage to succeed. Or muddle through?

animo non astutia
AHN-ih-moh nohn ahs-TOO-tih-ah
by courage, not by cunning

Another splendid motto for those who see themselves as brave and virtuous. How admirable are our qualities, at least in our own eyes. (See also ANIMO ET FIDE.)

animus furandi
AHN-ih-muus fuu-RAHN-dee
the intention of stealing

A legal phrase defining the mind-set of a person found guilty of stealing. "He said he acted on impulse, but clearly he broke into the house with *animus furandi.*"

animus meminisse horret
AHN-ih-muus MEH-mih-nihs-seh HAWR-ret
I can't bear to think of it

A locution from Virgil, literally "my soul shudders to remember," useful for anyone who has had terrible experiences and says he does not wish to tell others about them— or, more often, for one who is about to launch into a gory description of what he experienced.

anni nubiles
AHN-nee NOO-bih-lehs
age of consent

The Latin phrase, literally "marriageable years," defining the age at which a person becomes legally competent to consent to marriage or to sexual intercourse.

ante lucem
AHN-teh LOO-kem
just before daybreak

Literally "before light," the moments *ante lucem* precede "first light" or "dawn," in Latin **aurora** (ow-ROH-rah).

ante tubam trepidat
AHN-teh TOO-bahm TREH-pih-daht
he's wounded before a shot is fired

Anyone who has had first-hand knowledge of fear in battle knows it is not uncommon to begin to shake—or worse—even before the first gun is fired. In Roman times, the sounding of a battle trumpet signaled the start of serious business. *Ante tubam trepidat*, thus, suggests a soldier who becomes frightened before a battle begins, literally "he is alarmed before the trumpet (sounds)." And who can blame the unfortunate fellow?

ante victoriam ne canas triumphum
AHN-teh wee-KTOH-rih-ahm nay KAH-nahs tree-UUM-fuum
don't count your chickens before they're hatched

Very good advice for finalists in a tennis match: there's many a slip between Davis Cup and lip. Or, as Roman realists knew, when they said "do not sing your triumph before the victory." And let's all recall the wise words attributed to Yogi Berra, "It ain't over till it's over."

antiqua homo virtute ac fide
ahn-TEE-kwah HAW-moh wihr-TOO-teh ahk FIH-day
they don't make them like that no more

Terence characterizing a person of estimable character as "a man of the old-time virtue and good faith." In other words, a gentleman of the old school.

a posse ad esse
ah PAWS-seh ahd ES-seh
from possibility to actuality

A good motto for a firm of architects who provide service from initial drawings through completed structure, who might say, "We see our projects through *a posse ad esse.*" And the clients of the firm might one day say, "The entire procedure was a mess *a posse ad esse.*"

apparatus belli
ahp-pah-RAH-tuus BEL-lee
the apparatus of war

This term includes everything needed for war, from uniforms to food to guns to ammunition to all the rest.

apparent rari nantes in gurgite vasto
ahp-PAH-rent RAH-rih NAHN-tehs in GUUR-gih-teh WAHS-toh
a gem or two buried in a pile of manure

Virgil's metaphor, literally "a few appear (to be) swimming in a vast flood," used to describe a poor literary work offering a few worthwhile thoughts but obscuring them in an ocean of unnecessary words.

a principio
ah prin-KEE-pih-oh
from the beginning

aquilam volare doces
AH-kwih-lahm waw-LAH-reh DAW-kehs
you're teaching an eagle to fly

We are being told not to do what does not have to be done. Anyone who has seen an eagle on the wing knows it needs no flight training. (See also DELPHINUM NATARE DOCES.)

aquila non capit muscas
AH-kwih-lah nohn KAH-pit MUUS-kahs
I'm too important to bother with small fry

Anyone—or any nation—with an inflated self-concept may turn aside interruptions—or threats—with this locution, "an eagle doesn't catch flies." Bullies, on the other hand, spend all their time catching flies. And great nations periodically flex their muscles at the expense of tiny nations, at the same time avoiding conflict that may prove embarrassing or costly.

arcana imperii
ahr-KAH-nah im-PEH-rih-ee
state secrets

This phrase translates literally as "the secrets (or mysteries) of empire (or government)." Unfortunately, it is the habit of governments to classify everything as secret.

ardentia verba
ahr-DEN-tee-ah WEHR-bah
glowing language

More literally "burning words," but however *ardentia verba* is translated, you can be sure you'll recognize and appreciate such words when you encounter them.

arenae mandas semina
ah-RAY-nī MAHN-dahs SEH-mih-nah
you're attempting the impossible

Any farmer knows better than to try to raise a crop in sand. *Arena mandas semina*, literally "you're sowing seeds in sand," tells all of us not to waste our energy on vain enterprises. (See also ARENA SINE CALCE and EX ARENA FUNICULUM NECTIS.)

arena sine calce
ah-RAY-nah SIH-neh KAHL-keh
sand without lime

A line of reasoning that does not hold together may be described as *arena sine calce*. The metaphor, used by Suetonius to characterize loose statements that have nothing to bind them together, alludes to the impossibility of creating a stable mixture of sand and water without lime or some other material that enables sand to hold together. (See also EX ARENA FUNICULUM NECTIS.)

argumenti causa
ahr-goo-MEN-tee KOW-sah
for the sake of argument

Also given as *argumenti gratia* (GRAH-tee-ah), with the same meaning—and don't you hate people who habitually argue *argumenti causa?*

arma in armatos sumere iura (or jura) sinunt
AHR-mah in ahr-MAH-tohs SOO-meh-reh YOO-rah SEE-nuunt
it's OK to shoot someone who's pointing a gun at you

Nations appear to need no excuse for making war, but here is one anyway, "the laws permit the taking up of arms against those (who are) armed." This precept has long been followed to an extreme by nations—and individuals—who undertake so-called preemptive strikes in the face of a perceived, often imaginary, threat.

arma pacis fulcra
AHR-mah PAH-kihs FUUL-krah
arms are the props of peace

It is easy to see why the Romans took this maxim to heart. After all, at the height of their power they had to manage an enormous empire and thus were always in danger of attack on their borders as well as having to remain alert in the face of possible internal threats. (See also ARMA TUENTUR PACEM.)

arma tuentur pacem
AHR-mah too-EN-tuur PAH-kem
arms guard peace

Another plug for the importance of maintaining strong military forces. Despite—because of?—the ever-increasing output and sale of guns in our century, armed hostilities are proliferating almost everywhere, leading one to wonder whether "arms guard peace" is an example of Orwellian doublespeak. (See ARMA PACIS FULCRA.)

asinus ad lyram
AH-sih-nuus ahd LIHR-ahm
an ass at the lyre

A strong characterization applied to anyone totally devoid of appreciation or talent for anything artistic, for example, in music someone with a tin ear, in art someone with no eye for beauty.

asinus asino, et sus sui pulcher
AH-sih-nuus AH-sih-noh et soos SOO-ee PUUL-kehr
there's someone for everybody

This observation, "an ass is beautiful to an ass, and a pig to a pig," may not appear to be a felicitous way of alluding to people and the way they appear to one another, but it is comforting to believe that beauty may really be in the eyes of the beholder.

a teneris annis
ah TEH-neh-rihs AHN-nihs
from tender years

at spes non fracta
aht spays nohn FRAH-ktah
you can't keep a good man down

An apt phrase, literally "but hope is not shattered," for those who go on courageously and relentlessly in the face of extreme hardship. And there are such people. Consider this stanza from the poem "Invictus," (Latin in-WEE-ktuus, English in-VIK-təs, "unbeaten") by the 19th-century English poet William Ernest Henley:

> In the fell clutch of circumstance,
> I have not winced nor cried aloud;
> Under the bludgeonings of chance
> My head is bloody, but unbowed.

(See also INVICTUS MANEO.)

auctor pretiosa facit
OW-ktawr preh-tih-OH-sah FAH-kit
the giver makes (the gift) precious

For a fuller form of this saccharine observation, see ACCEPTISSIMA SEMPER MUNERA SUNT AUCTOR QUAE PRETIOSA FACIT.

audacia pro muro habetur
ow-DAH-kee-ah proh MOO-roh HAH-beh-tuur
there's nothing like a brave front

Anyone or any nation faced with an imminent threat knows that there are three ways to respond: Look tough and ready for combat yourself, fall on your knees and beg for mercy, or be brave and willing to compromise. In this maxim, literally "audacity serves as a defense," from Sallust, a 1st-century B.C. Roman historian, we are advised to adopt the first stance—I am ready for you, and you will pay a price for any act of aggression you undertake.

audacter calumniare semper aliquid haeret
ow-DAH-ktehr kah-luum-nih-AH-reh SEM-pehr AH-lih-kwid HĪ-ret
talk about negative campaigning!

This advice, "slander boldly, something always sticks," goes way back in time. And, for the slanderer, has more often than not been proved effective. So while our century has had its share of shameless lying, we certainly didn't invent the technique. (See also AUDACTER TE VENDITA SEMPER ALIQUID HAERET.)

audacter et sincere
ow-DAH-ktehr et sin-KAY-reh
boldly and frankly

A good motto to emblazon on a coat of arms. But not always a way to make friends and influence people.

audacter te vendita semper aliquid haeret
ow-DAH-ktehr tay WEN-dih-tah SEM-pehr AH-lih-kwid HĪ-ret
if you don't blow your own horn, who will?

Advice, "praise yourself boldly, something always sticks," that frequently is advanced by modern press agents. (See AUDACTER CALUMNIARE SEMPER ALIQUID HAERET.)

audax et cautus
OW-dahks et KOW-tuus
bold and wary

A motto incorporating the idea that one ought to move ahead fearlessly, but with a dash of caution. (See AUDE SAPERE.)

aude sapere
OW-day SAH-peh-reh
dare to be wise

Also translated as "dare to think independently." It takes strength of character to think independently, for example, to spurn well-intentioned advice from parents and less than well-intentioned advice from imprudent friends. Also given as SAPERE AUDE.

audi vide tace si vis vivere in pace
OW-dee WIH-day TAH-kay see wihs WEE-weh-reh in PAH-kay
hear no evil, see no evil, speak no evil

The wise person knows that there are times when one must speak up and times when it is better to keep one's own counsel. The advice given in this proverb, "hear, see, be silent if you wish to live in peace," teaches us the safe way—yet not always the most honorable way—to conduct ourselves. What this proverb does not tell us is how to know when to talk and when not to talk.

auribus teneo lupum
OW-rih-buus TEH-nay-oh LOO-puum
I've got a tiger by the tail

Anyone facing a problem for which there is no good solution may say *auribus teneo lupum*, "I'm holding a wolf by the ears." Thus, I cannot hold on forever, and I cannot let go—either action will leave me at the mercy of the beast. As the wise reader knows, the way out of this dilemma is to avoid getting into it.

aut amat aut odit mulier nihil est tertium
owt AH-maht owt OH-deet MOO-lee-ehr NIH-hil est TEHR-tih-uum
why can't they just be friends?

Talk about stereotypes! This is one of those marvelous insights—"a woman either loves or hates, there is no third way"—that must have endeared the men of ancient Rome to women, and it is still bothering women today.

aut mors aut victoria
owt mawrs owt wee-KTOH-rih-ah
either death or victory

Like American football coaches—whose employment con-
tracts depend on the ability to produce victories, not sports-
men—Roman generals weren't kidding when they sent their
troops out to do battle. This stirring battle cry is also given as
aut vincere aut mori (owt WIN-keh-reh owt MAW-ree, "either
to conquer or to die." (See also VINCERE AUT MORI.)

aut non tentaris aut perfice
owt nohn TEHN-tah-rihs owt pehr-FIH-keh
don't start anything you can't finish

This advice, literally "either don't attempt it or else finish
it," is intended to teach us good work habits. But while we
should not habitually leave things half done, isn't it better to
abandon an idea that shows sure signs of eventual failure than
to carry it through to the bitter end?

aut prodesse volunt aut delectare poetae
owt proh-DEHS-seh WAW-luunt owt deh-leh-KTAH-reh
paw-AY-tī
poets want either to profit or to please

Horace made this interesting observation in his epistolary
poem *Ars Poetica* (ahrs paw-AY-tih-kah, "The Art of Poetry").
Good to know that poets had both feet on the ground way
back in the 1st century B.C.

aut vitam aut culpam
owt WEE-tahm owt KUUL-pahm
just behave yourself

When someone is given a so-called lifetime appointment—
usually to a high judicial post—the appointment is not
intended to be entirely unconditional. Thus, the phrase *aut
vitam aut culpam*, literally "for life or until misconduct," may
be made part of the official notice of appointment.

auxilium ab alto
owk-SIH-lih-uum ahb AHL-toh
help from on high

a verbis ad verbera
ah WEHR-bees ahd WEHR-beh-rah
one thing leads to another

When a friendly discussion leads to strong disagreement and finally to fisticuffs, it has gone *a verbis ad verbera*, literally "from words to blows."

B

barbae tenus sapientes
BAHR-bī TEH-nuus sah-pee-EN-tehs
know-it-alls

Literally "men wise as far as a beard (makes them appear wise)." Worthy of pity or contempt are people—usually men—who pretend to knowledge they do not have. *Barbae tenus sapientes*, which evokes the image of young men who affect beards to make them look older and wiser, gives us a welcome phrase for referring to such men.

basis virtutum constantia
BAH-sihs wihr-TOO-tuum kawn-STAHN-tee-ah
just keep at it

Forget about Mozart, John Stuart Mill, and all the other famous child prodigies. If you're old enough to read this book, you're already too old to make it big in childhood. So what to do? *Basis virtutum constantia*, literally "steadiness is the pedestal of excellence," gives us the clue: Never stop trying to achieve whatever it is you really want to achieve.

beatus ille qui procul negotiis
beh-AH-tuus EEL-leh kwee PROH-kuul neh-GOH-tee-ees
move to Vermont

Horace praising the joys of living in the country, "happy the man who lives far away from the cares of business." In the 20th century, an entire generation of bright young people heeded his advice and settled down happily to bucolic careers in macramé, pottery, belt-making, organic farming, and the like—and a few years later entered law school or took MBAs.

bellum internecinum
BEHL-luum in-tehr-neh-KEE-nuum
a murderous war

More usually called "a war of extermination." For more on this distasteful subject, see AD INTERNECIONEM.

bellum lethale
BEHL-luum leh-TAH-leh
a deadly war

bellum nec timendum nec provocandum
BEHL-luum nek tih-MEN-duum nek proh-woh-KAHN-duum
don't run from or invite war

A Roman view of war, literally "war is neither to be feared nor to be provoked," that suggests a gung-ho mindset combined with enough good sense to make war seem almost acceptable. But doesn't it smack of advice that might be given by the too-old-to-be-drafted to the too-young-to-vote? (See also DULCE BELLUM INEXPERTIS.)

bellum omnium in omnes
BEHL-luum in AWM-nee-uum in AWM-nays
run for the hills

Talk about war! *Bellum omnium in omnes* is the big one, literally "the war of all against all."

belua multorum capitum
BAY-loo-ah muul-TAWR-uum KAH-pih-tuum
the multitude

Horace, in a far from democratic moment, denigrating the vast number of ordinary people by calling them "the monster of many heads."

bene decessit
BEH-neh deh-KES-siht
the way to go

When someone has died a natural death or has died under honorable circumstances, we may say of him or her, *bene decessit*, "he (or she) has died well."

bene est tentare
BEH-neh est ten-TAH-reh
there's nothing to lose

When your cause is just and you have some chance of achieving success, follow this advice, literally "it is as well to try."

bene exeat
BEH-neh EH-ksay-aht
a good character reference

This phrase, "let him (or her) go forth well," is the Roman equivalent of a personal or institutional letter of recommendation.

beneficium invito non datur
beh-neh-FIH-kee-uum in-WEE-toh nohn DAH-tuur
I thought it was just a gift

This maxim, literally "a benefit cannot be bestowed on an unwilling person," advises us to question whether an exceptional act of generosity carries with it an unstated expectation that something—perhaps something illicit—is expected in return, that is, **quid pro quo** (kwid proh kwoh), literally "something for something."

bene merenti
BEH-neh meh-REN-tee
to the well-deserving

A phrase that may be used when bestowing a gift or award: "Today we are gathered to pay homage to our retiring leader *bene merenti*." The plural is **bene merentibus** (meh-REN-tih-buus).

bene meritus
BEH-neh MEH-rih-tuus
having well deserved

An alternative form of BENE MERENTI. The plural form is **bene meriti** (MEH-rih-tee).

bene nati, bene vestiti, et mediocriter docti
BEH-neh NAH-tee BEH-neh WEHS-tih-tee et meh-dee-AW-krih-tehr DAW-ktee
don't judge a book by its cover

An apt characterization of a second-rate mind, literally "well born, well dressed, and so-so in learning." (See also NE FRONTI CREDE.)

bene orasse est bene studuisse
BEH-neh oh-RAHS-seh est BEH-neh stuu-doo-EES-seh
to have prayed well is to have striven well

bene qui coniecit vatem hunc perhibebo optimum
BEH-neh kwee kawn-YEH-keet WAH-tem huunk pehr-
HIH-beh-boh AW-ptih-muum
watch out for economists and racetrack touts

Cicero offering us cynical and wise words on those who make their livings by predicting future events, literally "I shall always assert that he who guesses best is the best prophet."

bene qui latuit bene vixit
BEH-neh kwee LAH-too-it BEH-neh WEE-ksit
avoid the limelight

Ovid telling us that if we want happiness, we should not pursue fame, more literally "well has he lived who has lived in obscurity." (See also CAPUT INTER NUBILA CONDIT.)

bene vale
BEH-neh WAH-lay
farewell

Also given as **bene vale vobis** (WOH-bees, "to you").

benigno numine
beh-NIH-gnoh NOO-mih-neh
with a favoring providence

Horace has given us a self-effacing way of explaining whatever success we manage to achieve: "I made it to where I am *benigno numine*." The phrase may also serve as a modest way of requesting divine assistance: "*Benigno numine*, we shall succeed in our search."

bibere venenum in auro
BEE-beh-reh weh-NEH-nuum in OW-roh
it's a mistake to flaunt your wealth

This intriguing phrase, "to drink poison from a golden cup," suggests that in Roman times the rich—those who drank from golden cups—were the likely targets of poisoners and other felons. Why would anyone bother to do in the poor, who drank from cups of clay? Who would profit from poisoning a poor person?

bis
bihs
twice

Also translated as "a second time" or "repeat." We also know "bis" as a Latin term taken into Italian and then adopted in English as the equivalent of "encore!"

bis peccare in bello non licet
bihs pehk-KAH-reh in BEHL-loh nohn LIH-keht
you're allowed one and only one mistake

While many of us may believe that wars are won by strokes of strategic and tactical brilliance, it is more likely that wars are won by the side that makes fewer strategic and tactical blunders. The military maxim given here, literally "to make a mistake twice in war is not allowable," recognizes the validity of this assertion. One mistake? Probably not decisive. But two? Don't ask.

bis pueri senes
bihs POO-eh-ree SEH-nehs
second childhood

This disagreeable observation, literally "old men are children twice," describes the condition known as senility. The same thought also appears in a singular form, **senex bis puer** (SEH-neks bihs POO-ehr, "an old man is twice a boy"). Whether plural or singular, let's hope the geneticists and gerontologists one day soon will do something marvelous to prevent or reverse the unhappy condition.

bis vincit qui se vincit in victoria
bihs WIN-kit kwee say WIN-kit in wih-KTAWR-ee-ah
don't crow

Publilius Syrus giving us sound advice, "he conquers twice who conquers himself in the hour of victory." First of all, nobody—least of all a runner-up—likes boasters. Secondly, so cyclical is the nature of human experience that today's defeated person or nation can be counted on to become tomorrow's winner.

blandae mendacia linguae
BLAHN-dī men-DAH-kee-ah LIN-gwī
lies of a flattering tongue

Two hundred years ago, Jonathan Swift called flattery "the food of fools." Thus, whereas we all know "flattery will get you nowhere" as a rejoinder to the blandishments of a person striving to gain some favor, we also know that flattery is wonderfully effective. Witness the ironic "flattery will get you everything." All we can hope for is that *blandae mendacia linguae* will alert you and me to be on guard next time we are exposed to flattery.

bona opinio hominum tutior pecunia est
BAW-nah aw-PEE-nee-oh HAW-mih-nuum TOO-tee-awr peh-KOO-nee-ah est
guard your reputation as your life

Publilius Syrus telling us how valuable are our reputations, literally "the good opinion of men is safer than money." We've been given this advice many times over the centuries. For example, Shakespeare, in *Othello*, had Iago say, "But he that filches from me my good name...makes me poor indeed." This lesson, alas, is not absorbed by all our political leaders until after they have seriously damaged their reputations, and one scandal seems only to lead to the next. Will we ever learn?

bonis quod bene fit haud perit
BAW-nees kwawd BEH-neh feet howd PEH-rit
whatever is done for good men is never lost

An observation of Plautus, assuring us that we will always be remembered for our acts of kindness.

boni principii finis bonus
BAW-nee preen-KIH-pih-ee FEE-nis BAW-nuus
start off on the right foot

Literally "from a good beginning a good ending." A 14th-century English proverb conveys the same message, generally given as "a good beginning makes a good ending." In short, everyone knows this observation is valid. The clear implication is, however, that when we start off on the wrong foot, everything can be counted on to go wrong.

bonis nocet quisquis pepercerit malis
BAW-nees NAW-ket KWIHS-kwihs peh-PEHR-keh-rit MAH-lees
stop coddling criminals

People who seek support for harsh judicial systems will welcome this proverb from Publilius Syrus on the question of public safety, literally "whoever spares the wicked harms the good." This is the kind of stuff that leads to the sentencing practice called "three strikes and you're out." Which means "three major criminal convictions and you're in—for life." (See also QUI PARCIT NOCENTIBUS INNOCENTES PUNIT.)

bonum commune
BAW-nuum kawm-MOO-neh
the common good

bonus dux bonum reddit militem
BAW-nuus duuks BAW-nuum RED-dit MEE-lih-tem
a good leader makes a good soldier

bonus vir semper tiro
BAW-nuus wihr SEM-pehr TEE-roh
always willing to learn

This maxim, "a good man is always a beginner," teaches that advancement to high position does not mean the end of learning. Rather, there is always something to be learned no matter how exalted or powerful someone is. A good motto for a CEO's desk.

bos in lingua
bohs in LEEN-gwah
a reason for holding one's tongue

This splendid trope, literally "an ox on the tongue," is used to indicate a weighty reason for silence. "Why are they so quiet?" "Surely they have *bos in lingua.*"

bracchium civile
BRAHK-kee-uum see-WEE-leh
the civil arm *or* civil power

Of the government, that is. Also given as **bracchium saeculare** (sī-kuu-LAH-reh), with the same meaning.

brevi manu
BREH-wee MAH-noo
offhand

The literal translation is "with a short hand."

brevis esse laboro, obscurus fio
BREH-wees ES-seh lah-BAW-roh awb-SKOO-ruus FEE-oh
in trying to be concise, I become obscure

Horace, in *Ars Poetica*, instructing writers that it is difficult to achieve brevity without sacrificing clarity. Thus Thoreau's line: "Not that the story need be long, but it will take a long while to make it short."

brevis oratio penetrat caelum
BREH-wihs oh-RAH-tee-oh PEH-neh-traht KĪ-luum
a brief prayer reaches heaven

And by extension, brevity in any message is both welcome and effective.

C

caecus amor sui
KĪ-kuus AH-mawr SOO-ee
blind love of self

We have all grown up knowing that love is blind, enabling us to overlook undesirable traits in our beloveds—surely a happy condition. Here, however, Horace tells us that even self-love can be blind—surely not a happy condition. Narcissists, beware.

caelitus mihi vires
KĪ-lih-tuus MIH-hih WEE-rays
my strength is from heaven

Worth believing if you don't stretch it too far.

Caesar non supra grammaticos
KĪ-sahr nohn SUU-prah grahm-MAH-tih-kohs
every last one of us should speak and write correctly

This dictum, "Caesar is not above the grammarians," is taken to show the deep respect that Romans had for their language and literature—even the Emperor was expected to handle words with care. Suetonius wrote of an incident in which Tiberius, a 1st-century Roman emperor, made a grammatical error in a speech. When one of his favorites said it couldn't have been an error because Tiberius was the one who used the locution in dispute, a grammarian replied TU ENIM, CAESAR, CIVITATEM DARE POTES HOMINIBUS, VERBA NON POTES (too EH-nim KĪ-sahr kih-wih-TAH-tem DAH-reh PAW-tehs haw-MIH-nih-buus WEHR-bah nohn PAW-tehs), "you, Caesar, can designate men as citizens, but not make words." Two good thoughts— *Caesar non supra* and TU ENIM, CAESAR—to interject when modern American political leaders massacre the English language.

calceus maior subvertit
KAHL-kay-uus MAH-yawr suub-WEHR-tit
don't get too big for your britches

This metaphorical warning, "a shoe too large trips," may be directed at overly aggressive power-grabbers as well as at entrepreneurs with big eyes. It suggests that enterprises may fall apart because they become too large and unwieldy. Thus, when an already huge conglomerate goes after its umpteenth acquisition, the prudent financial adviser may cite *calceus maior subvertit.*

callida iunctura (or junctura)
KAHL-lee-dah yuun-KTUUR-ah
skillful workmanship

This phrase of Horace may also be taken as "skillful joining," with "joining" referring to the work of a cabinetmaker. More broadly, *callida iunctura* may be used as an expression of admiration for any activity accomplished with great skill.

calvo turpius est nihil comato
KAHL-woh TUUR-pee-uus est NIH-hil koh-MAH-toh
don't pretend to be more than you are

One growth industry in our century thrives on developing lotions intended to encourage hair to sprout on men's heads, on transplanting hair when the lotions don't work, and on supplying wigs when other measures fail. Martial's observation to Romans, freely rendered as "there's nothing more unsightly than a bald man with a wig," is directed at those who pretend—whether out of vanity or the desire to deceive—to be more than they really are. The adjective *comatus* translates literally as "longhaired," so *calvo turpius est nihil comato* may also be taken as "there's nothing more unsightly than a long-haired bald man."

candida pax
KAHN-dih-dah pahks
radiant peace

Ovid characterizing peace among nations, the blessed condition following cessation of warfare. The adjective *candida* is translated variously as "white," "bright," "beautiful," "fair," and "clothed in white," as well as "radiant." Take your choice. 'Tis a cessation devoutly to be wished.

candide et constanter
KAHN-dih-deh et kawn-STAHN-tehr
frankly and firmly

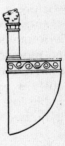

canis in praesepi
KAHN-ihs in PRĪ-seh-pee
dog in the manger

This expression is traceable to Aesop's fable in which a dog stations itself near a pile of hay in order to prevent an ox from eating the hay even though the dog itself doesn't eat hay. Thus, *canis in praesepi*, more accurately "dog in the stable," characterizes the disagreeable person who thinks, "If I can't enjoy something, I'll make sure no one else does." Try using the phrase when next you find yourself in a theater sitting next to a potato-chip cruncher who hates the movie being shown and doesn't miss an opportunity to ruin the pleasure of the rest of us.

canis timidus vehementius latrat quam mordet
KAH-nihs TIH-mih-duus way-heh-MEN-tee-uus LAH-
traht kwahm MAWR-det
a cowardly dog barks more than it bites

There's accurate insight in this Roman proverb. The trouble
is that postal workers don't know whether a barking dog is
cowardly. And when we apply the proverb to the threats of
human bullies, we can only hope that blusterers won't resort
to blows. Maybe, but don't count on it.

cantabit vacuus coram latrone viator
kahn-TAH-bit WAH-koo-uus KOH-rahm lah-TRAW-neh
WEE-ah-tawr
a penniless person has nothing to lose

Juvenal telling us "the traveler with an empty purse will
sing before a robber." Those of us who live in crime-ridden
cities know better than to take Juvenal literally today. The
modern mugger hates nothing more than being told his target
has no money at all. Thus the common practice of always carrying an amount of folding money on one's person—enough
to satisfy a wretch we encounter, but not so large that the
inevitable loss will be sorely felt. We surely have advanced in
civility in two millennia.

cantilenam eandem canis
kahn-tih-LAY-nahm ay-AHN-dem KAHN-ihs
you're singing the same old song

Terence's way of saying "there you go again."

capiat qui capere possit
KAH-pee-aht kwee KAH-peh-reh PAWS-sit
let him take who can take

capistrum maritale
kah-PEES-truum mah-rih-TAH-leh
the woes of matrimony

Juvenal, in a disillusioned view of marriage, speaking literally of "the matrimonial halter." If the reader is not certain of the intended sense of "halter," let it be known that *capistrum* can also be translated as "muzzle." Need we go further?

captantes capti sumus
kah-PTAHN-tays KAH-ptee SUU-muus
the tables have been turned

A marvelous idiom, literally "we catchers have been caught," more loosely rendered as "the biters are bitten." All by way of giving the lie to the American adage "never try to con a con man."

captatio benevolentiae
kah-PTAH-tee-oh beh-neh-waw-LEN-tee-ī
laying it on thick

This expression, literally "catching at goodwill," more idiomatically "currying favor," encapsulates the central tactic of the sycophant.

captus nidore culinae
KAH-ptuus nih-DOH-reh kuu-LEE-nī
irresistibly sucked in

Juvenal's colorful way of explaining loss of willpower in the face of great temptation, literally "captivated by the aroma of the kitchen." We can conjure up any number of situations in which the metaphor can be applied, always certain that it will surpass the pedestrian "I just couldn't help myself."

caput inter nubila condit
KAH-puut IN-tehr NOO-bih-lah KAWN-dit
she hides her head among the clouds

Who is she that hides? The line is from Virgil, who had the personified "fame" in mind as the subject of the verb *condit*. And, for most of us, fame never does emerge from behind the clouds to bathe us in glory. Instead, we labor on in obscurity, awaiting our fifteen minutes of celebrity. (See also BENE QUI LATUIT BENE VIXIT.)

caput lupinum
KAH-puut loo-PEE-nuum
sign of the outlaw

In Old English law, a person who was declared an outlaw—*caput lupinum*, literally "a wolf's head"—could legally be hunted down and killed by anyone who came upon him. The words decreeing outlawry were **caput gerat** (GEH-raht) **lupinum**, "let him wear the wolf's head," that is, treat him as you would a wild beast.

carent quia vate sacro
KAH-rent KWEE-ah WAH-teh SAH-kroh
golden words are needed

Horace's phrase, literally "because they lack an inspired bard," explaining that a nation will be forgotten if it is not blessed with the presence of a gifted poet to record the accomplishments of its people.

caret initio et fine
KAH-ret ih-NEE-tee-oh et FEE-neh
it lacks beginning and end

Literary critics reviewing a less-than-perfect work need say no more.

carmen triumphale
KAHR-men tree-uum-FAH-leh
a song of triumph

carmina morte carent
KAHR-mih-nah MAWR-teh KAH-rent
songs are exempt from death

> A line from Ovid asserting that good poetry never dies.

carpent tua poma nepotes
KAHR-pent TOO-ah PAWM-ah neh-PAW-tehs
plan for the future

> In suggesting literally that "your grandsons will gather your apples," Virgil is telling us that hard work and careful management of our resources will pay off long after we are gone. But *nepotes*, "grandsons," may also be translated as "descendants" or as "spendthrifts." The third translation of *nepotes* is enough to send chills up our spines, making us wonder whether we blunder in planning carefully for future generations, who can be expected to waste the resources passed on to them.

carpere et colligere
KAHR-peh-reh et kawl-LIH-geh-reh
to pluck and gather

cassis tutissima virtus
KAHS-sihs too-TIHS-sih-mah WIHR-tuus
an honest man need fear nothing

> This proverb, literally "virtue is the securest helmet," suggests the efficacy of playing the game of life by the rules. What it fails to recognize is that the rules may change, depending on who writes and administers the rules.

castigo te non quod odio habeam, sed quod amem
KAHS-tih-goh tay nohn kwawd AW-dee-oh HAH-bay-ahm sed kwawd AH-mem

this hurts me more than it hurts you

Before administering corporal punishment, parents in two-parent families have traditionally incanted these magical words, literally "I punish you not because I hate, but because I love." In Rome this formula was invoked by a person about to administer a flogging to an unfortunate wretch found guilty of crime. Now it is intended to help a child survive the experience and—in some mysterious way—see a whipping or spanking as so painful for the parent as to suggest that perhaps the child is really punishing the parent.

casus fortuitus
KAHS-uus fawr-too-EE-tuus

a matter of chance

In addition to "a matter of chance," *casus fortuitus* is variously translated, for example, as "an inevitable accident" and "a fortuitous occurrence." The final translation is the least satisfactory for the modern reader who may employ the English word "fortuitous" as a synonym for "fortunate." In the best modern usage, a fortuitous occurrence is not intended to denote a fortunate occurrence. Although many writers and speakers may use "fortunate" and "fortuitous" interchangeably, they cannot alter the meaning of the Latin *fortuitus*, whose meaning can best be seen by citing yet another appropriate translation of *casus fortuitus*, "an act of God." This English phrase, often employed in insurance policies, denotes an accident over which people have no control—lightning, hurricane, flood, and the like. Surely, none of these phenomena can be considered fortunate.

casus necessitatus
KAH-suus neh-kes-sih-TAH-tuus

a case of necessity

causa latet, vis est notissima
KOW-sah LAH-tet wees est noh-TIHS-sih-mah
the cause is hidden, its force is very well known

An observation of Ovid applicable to many occurrences and human proclivities. Consider, for example, the rapid growth of juvenile criminal behavior in modern times. Despite the plethora of scholarly and simplistic explanations offered by experts and nonexperts, juvenile criminality is still an instance of *causa latet, vis est notissima.*

cavendo tutus
kah-WEN-doh TOO-tuus
keep your wits about you

Surely an apt prescription, literally "safe by taking heed," for those who live in potentially dangerous places: "Remember, whenever you go out, *cavendo tutus.*"

cave ne cadas
KAH-way nay KAH-dahs
the bigger they come, the harder they fall

This advice, literally "beware lest thou fall," is most apt for anyone who has achieved a position of some prominence, whether real or imagined. Underlying this locution is the thought that people who rise may later fall, and so it behooves the risers to be nice to the non-risers they pass on the way, for the risers may meet the non-risers again on the way down, when the risers themselves have become fallers. And, of course, the higher people rise, the more people they pass on the way up. The jocular "the bigger they come, the harder they fall" is a commonly used English version of *cave ne cadas* but has a different ultimate meaning. "The bigger they come. . . " alludes to how far a knocked-out prizefighter will fall on his way to the canvas. The saying is variously attributed to well-known prizefighters of the past boasting that they fought and beat bigger and heavier opponents. (See also CELSAE GRAVIORE CASU DECIDUNT TURRES.)

cave tibi a cane muto et aqua silenti
KAH-way TIH-bih ah KAH-neh MOO-toh et AH-kwah
sih-LEN-tih
beware of a silent dog and still water

No one knows the underlying nature of either, so the wise person keeps his distance.

celeritas et veritas
keh-LEH-rih-tahs et WAY-rih-tahs
promptness and truth

celsae graviore casu decidunt turres
KEL-sī grah-wee-AWR-eh KAH-soo deh-KEE-duunt
TUUR-rehs
the bigger they come, the harder they fall

Horace advising caution, literally "lofty towers fall with a greater crash," for those on the way up in their careers. This is the same advice given by CAVE NE CADAS, "beware lest you fall," but Horace put the message metaphorically, as befits a poet. Incidentally, *celsae*, "lofty," may also be translated as "haughty" when applied to people. (For a contrasting thought, see HUMILIS NEC ALTE CADERE NEC GRAVITER POTEST.)

censor librorum
KEN-sawr lih-BRAWR-uum
a censor of books

An occupational title still to be found in modern times.

censor morum
KEN-sawr MOH-ruum
a censor

Not someone you especially want to know, literally "the regulator of morals," but someone the Romans had to be wary of. Another phrase with the same meaning is **custos** (KUUS-tohs, "guardian") **morum**.

certamina divitiarum
kehr-TAH-mih-nah dih-wih-tee-AH-ruum
strivings after wealth

Horace's phrase for the all-consuming struggles—*certamina* also means "battles"—for wealth that dominate the lives of too many people and prevent them from focusing on more laudable and more humane pursuits.

certaminis gaudia
kehr-TAH-mih-nihs GOW-dee-ah
the joys of battle

Yes, Virginia, there were Romans who relished a good fight. (See also GAUDIUM CERTAMINIS for the singular of *certaminis gaudia*.)

certum voto pete finem
KEHR-tuum WOH-toh PEH-teh FEE-nem
don't reach for the moon

Realistic advice from Horace, literally "seek a definite limit to your desire." And then be satisfied with what you achieve. What would Horace have thought of modern financial moguls and baseball players whose annual incomes exceed the gross national products of some nations?

cetera quis nescit?
KAY-teh-rah kwihs NEH-skit
who does not know the rest?

Ovid's phrase giving us a way to terminate a recounting of an opponent's misdeeds by suggesting that there is a lot more to tell, but everybody already knows all about it. At least that is what is implied.

cicatrix manet
KIH-kah-treeks MAH-net
the memory lingers on

Human psyches being what they are, we may apparently recover from a bad experience, but *cicatrix manet*, literally "the scar remains." And what kinds of bad experiences are these that scar us? Being thrashed by a schoolyard bully, being jilted by a sweetheart, failing to make the varsity football team, being laid off by an employer—the list is endless. (See also ETIAM SANATO VULNERE CICATRIX MANET.)

cineri gloria sera venit
KIH-neh-rih GLOH-ree-ah SEH-rah WAY-nit
glory paid to one's ashes comes too late

Martial's epigram telling us not to wait until someone is dead before praising him.

circuitus verborum
kihr-KOO-ih-tuus wehr-BOH-ruum
a circumlocution

circulus in definiendo
KIHR-kuu-luus in day-fin-ee-EN-doh
a circular definition

This phrase, literally "a circle in defining," is the particular concern of the lexicographer. A circular definition is a faulty form of definition, in which the definition includes the term being defined—a real no-no. Thus, even though anyone with even a rudimentary knowledge of English knows what the word "door" means, the definer of the word must struggle to accomplish the task ever mindful of the peril of *circulus in definiendo*. Consider, for example, the bravura performance of the scholars who wrote the great *Oxford English Dictionary*. Making certain to avoid *circulus in definiendo*, they defined "door" as "a movable barrier of wood or other material, consisting either of one piece, or of several pieces framed together, usually turning on hinges or sliding in a groove, and serving to close or open a passage into a building, room, etc."

circulus in probando
KIHR-kuu-luus in praw-BAHN-doh
circular reasoning

This term, literally "a circle in proving," is also called "reasoning in a circle." It denotes a faulty form of reasoning in which the conclusion itself is assumed as one of the premises. For example, consider "You can't expect poor people ever to rise out of poverty, because poverty cannot be overcome."

citius venit periculum cum contemnitur
KIH-tee-uus WAY-nit peh-REE-kuu-luum kuum kawn-TEM-nih-tuur
don't hide your head in the sand

Good advice to all, literally "danger comes sooner when it is not feared," and you ignore this advice at your own peril.

cito maturum, cito putridum
KIH-toh MAH-tuu-ruum KIH-toh POO-trih-duum
quickly ripe, quickly rotten

Fruit, economies, love affairs, novelists, business enterprises—and tennis players—should be permitted to develop slowly.

civis Romanus sum
KEE-wihs roh-MAH-nuus suum
Ich bin ein Berliner

President John F. Kennedy, alluding to Cicero's proud declaration—literally "I am a Roman citizen." Kennedy's implication paralleled that of Cicero: Citizens (Germans as well as Romans) have political rights, and those rights are not to be denied.

clarum et venerabile nomen
KLAH-ruum et weh-neh-RAH-bih-leh NOH-men
an illustrious and venerable name

A phrase from Lucan to use when extolling someone truly distinguished. He was recalling Pompey, the great Roman general and statesman. Anyone to whom this phrase is accurately applied is surely in good company.

clavam extorquere Herculi
KLAH-wahm eks-TAWR-keh-reh HEHR-koo-lee
to move mountains

A colorful way, literally "to wrest the club from Hercules," to describe a well-nigh impossible task that demands great courage as well as extraordinary strength.

cognatio movit invidiam
kaw-GNAH-tee-oh MAW-wit in-WIH-dee-ahm
kinship promotes ill feeling

Another indication that Roman families—not unlike some families today—did not enjoy uninterrupted good feelings. Perhaps members of a family get to know too much about one another. (See also ACERRIMA PROXIMORUM ODIA.)

colloquio iam tempus adest
kawl-LAW-kwee-oh yahm TEM-puus AHD-est
let's talk

Ovid telling us that "now the time for conversation is at hand."

colluvies vitiorem
kawl-LUU-wee-ays wih-tih-OH-rem
an unsavory collection

This phrase, literally "dregs of vice," provides an excellent characterization of any institution one may choose to denigrate—a state legislature, a municipal government, professional boxing, drug pushers, college athletic scholarship programs, etc.

colubrem in sinu fovere
kaw-LOO-brem in SIH-noo faw-WAY-reh
to cherish a serpent in one's bosom

This colorful phrase had its origin in Greek folklore. A farmer one morning picked up a frozen snake and put it into his bosom to warm it up. When the creature was revived by the warmth of the farmer's body, it promptly bit the farmer. Enough to make some of us turn away from a person in need.

columna bellica
kaw-LUUM-nah BEHL-lih-kah
war column *or* war memorial

comes iucundus (or jucundis) in via pro vehiculo est
KAW-mehs yoo-KUUN-duus in WEE-ah proh weh-HIH-kuu-loh est
a companion on the road is as good as a carriage

Publilius Syrus telling us that on a long journey pleasant company helps time pass.

comitas gentium
KAW-mih-tahs GEN-tee-uum
comity of nations

Also given as **comitas inter gentes** (IN-tehr GEN-tehs, "between nations"). Affability between nations is the basis for diplomacy.

commodum ex iniuria (or injuria) sua nemo habere debet

KAWM-maw-duum eks in-YUUR-ee-ah SOO-ah NAY-moh hah-BAY-reh DAY-bet

no one should profit from his own wrongdoing

A popular opinion in modern times.

commune periculum concordiam parit

kawm-MOO-neh peh-REE-kuu-luum kawn-KAWR-dee-ahm PAHR-it

common danger creates unity

Nothing like a good scare to get people to forget their petty differences and work together for the common good.

communis sensus

kawm-MOO-nihs SAYN-suus

common opinion

The best way for parties to a dispute to end their disagreement. Also taken as "common consent."

compendia dispendia

kawm-PEN-dee-ah dihs-PEHN-dee-ah

shortcuts are roundabout ways

This aphorism encourages care and thoroughness in any undertaking lest an urge to cut corners result in botched work and lead only to starting all over again. In a narrower sense, motorists who go out of their way to save time may in the long run lose time.

compesce mentem

kawm-PES-keh MEN-tem

control your temper

In literal translation, as "suppress feelings," this advice from Horace may not be sound from the point of view of mental health experts, but when taken to mean "control your temper," it cannot be faulted.

componere lites
kawm-POH-neh-reh LEE-tehs
to settle disputes

> See also TANTAS COMPONERE LITES

compos voti
KAWM-pohs WOH-tee
having gotten one's wish

concedo
kawn-KAY-doh
I concede

A term in logic employed to grant that an opponent's argument is superior to one's own. (See also MAIORI CEDO.)

concordia discors
kawn-KAWR-dee-ah DIHS-kawrs
discordant harmony

A marvelous oxymoron coined by Horace that today would be useful in referring to conditions prevalent in many nations of Central Europe, Africa, the Korean peninsula, and elsewhere. Modern democracies appear always to be practicing—and profiting from—a form of *concordia discors* that might be considered for so-called dysfunctional families.

confido et conquiesco
kawn-FEE-doh et kawn-kwee-EH-skoh
I trust and am at peace

coniunctis (or conjunctis) viribus
kawn-YUUN-ktihs WIH-ree-buus
in complete cooperation

This phrase, literally "with united powers," identifies the much-desired condition that a well organized enterprise strives for in order to succeed.

conquiescat in pace
kawn-kwee-EH-skaht in PAH-keh
may he (or she) rest in peace

This final thought is identical in meaning with the more familiar **requiescat** (reh-kwee-EH-skaht) **in pace**.

conscia mens recti
KOHN-skee-ah mehns REK-tee
someone who knows right from wrong

Ovid's phrase, literally "a mind conscious of rectitude."

conscientia mille testes
kohn-skee-EN-tee-ah MEE-leh TES-tehs
conscience is worth a thousand witnesses

But not in a court of justice.

consensus tollit errorem
kawn-SAYN-suus TAWL-lit ehr-ROH-rem
agreement removes uncertainty

Decisions are easy when all parties to a debate agree.

consequitur quodcunque petit
kohn-SEH-kwih-tuur kwawd-KUUN-kweh PEH-teet
he attains whatever he attempts

An admirable person.

consilio et animis
kohn-SIH-lee-oh et AH-nih-mees
by wisdom and courage

Another self-adulatory motto to emblazon on your family coat of arms—if you find it appropriate. (For additional mottoes, see the next three entries and AUDAX ET CAUTUS and AUDACITER ET SINCERE.)

consilio et prudentia
kohn-SIH-lee-oh et proo-DEN-tee-ah
by wisdom and prudence

consilio, non impetu
kohn-SIH-lee-oh nohn IM-peh-too
by deliberation *or* wisdom, not by impulse

constantia et virtute
kohn-STAHN-tee-ah et wihr-TOO-teh
by firmness and courage

consuetudo est optima interpres legum
kohn-soo-eh-TOO-doh est AW-ptih-mah in-TEHR-prehs LAY-guum
custom is the best interpreter of laws

When existing statutes are vague, or when no statutes apply to a matter at hand, justice is best served by considering the customs of a community. (See CONSUETUDO PRO LEGE SERVATUR.)

consuetudo loci observanda est
kohn-soo-eh-TOO-doh LAW-kī awb-sehr-WAHN-dah est
when in Rome, do as the Romans do

Good advice, literally "the custom of the place is to be observed," for any ancient or modern stranger in a strange land.

consuetudo pro lege servatur
kohn-soo-eh-TOO-doh proh LAY-geh sehr-WAH-tuur
custom is observed as law

This legal maxim reminds us that laws generally have their origin in local customs. (See also CONSUETUDO EST OPTIMA INTERPRES LEGUM.)

consuetudo quasi altera natura
kohn-soo-eh-TOO-doh KWAH-see AHL-teh-rah nah-TOO-rah
habit is, as it were, second nature

Caesar on the efficacy of routine.

contra felicem vix deus vires habet
KAWN-trah feh-LEE-kem wiks DAY-uus WIHR-ehs HAH-bet
don't bet against a crapshooter on a roll

Publilius Syrus telling us that "against a lucky man a god scarcely has power." Why buck the odds?

contra ius (or jus) gentium
KAWN-trah yoos GEHN-tee-uum
against the law of nations

contra malum mortis non est medicamen in hortis
KAWN-trah MAH-luum MAWR-tihs nohn est meh-dih-KAH-men in HAWR-tihs
no one wins out against death

A sure bet, literally "against the evil of death there is no remedy in the gardens." And if we are to take literally the last word of this observation—*hortis*, "in the gardens"—not even herbal remedies will do any good.

contra mundum
KAWN-trah MUUN-duum

against the world

Brave souls—at best dreamers, at worst fools—who stand *contra mundum* are those who defy prevailing opinion.

contra negantem principia non est disputandum
KAWN-trah neh-GAHN-tem preen-KIH-pee-ah nohn est dihs-puu-TAHN-duum

there's no arguing with one who denies first principles

This validity of this observation cannot be denied. Consider the incoherent rantings of people who ignore well-established facts and human experience to argue for their political or social agendas.

copia verborum
KOH-pee-ah wehr-BOH-ruum

prolixity

The condition of wordiness, literally "abundance of words," also given as **copia fandi** (FAHN-dee), "abundance of talk." Whichever phrase is used, this boring phenomenon must be stamped out. Readers and listeners of the world, unite!

cor ad cor loquitur
kawr ahd kawr LAW-kwih-tuur

heart speaks to heart

Surely there is no better way to speak than heart to heart. *Cor ad cor loquitur* was the motto of John Henry Newman, known usually as Cardinal Newman. He was a 19th-century Anglican theologian who converted to Catholicism in 1845 and in 1879 was made a cardinal. (See his epitaph, EX UMBRIS ET IMAGINIBUS IN VERITATEM.)

coram paribus
KOH-rahm PAH-rih-buus
before equals

In the democratic tradition, we expect that a jury trial will be held *coram paribus,* best translated as "before one's peers." Peers in this sense are persons having the same legal status as the person on trial. They are not required to be the equals of the person on trial in any other sense.

cor illi in genua decidet
kawr IL-lih in GEH-nuu-ah DAY-kih-det
he is scared stiff

Literally "his heart falls into his knees," and we all know that knees are said to shake when someone is extremely frightened.

cor ne edito
kawr nay AY-dee-toh
share your troubles with a pal or therapist

Excellent advice, literally "eat not thy heart," in a Latin translation of a phrase attributed to Pythagoras, the 6th-century B.C. Greek philosopher. Rather than eat your heart out in silence, he said, open up to someone you trust. You'll feel better.

corpora lente augescunt cite exstinguuntur
KAWR-paw-rah LEN-teh ow-GEH-skuunt KEE-teh ek-STEEN-gwuun-tuur
we grow slowly, die quickly

Tacitus making a depressing observation, literally "bodies are slow in growth, rapid in decay."

corpus valet sed aegrotat crumena
KAWR-puus WAH-let sed ī-GROH-taht kroo-MAY-nah
what good is health if you can't afford to enjoy it?

We are accustomed to hearing that health is better than wealth, but now we hear the complaint in *corpus valet sed aegrotat crumena* that "the body is well, but the purse is sick." The inference is clear: health without the money to enjoy it is not all it's cracked up to be.

corruptio optimi pessima
kawr-RUU-ptee-oh AW-ptih-mee PES-sih-mah
corruption of the best is worst

We express no surprise when bank tellers are caught with their hands in the cookie jar—we have learned to be forgiving with persons who probably are paid small salaries. But when, for example, a scientist, like Shakespeare's soldier "seeking the bubble reputation," is caught fudging experimental data—that is a different matter. It is in this spirit that we may understand *corruptio optimi pessima.*

corruptissima in republica plurimae leges
kawr-ruu-PTIHS-sih-mah in ray-POO-blih-kah PLOO-rih-mī LAY-gihs
the more corrupt the state, the more numerous the laws

Tacitus hit this one on the nose. Every time a government tries to strengthen its laws, the enemies of the state find new ways to cheat—with the assistance of clever lawyers, accountants, and lobbyists—which inevitably lead to more and more laws, and less and less observance of the laws. And so on.

crambe repetita
KRAHM-bay reh-peh-TEE-tah
warmed-over cabbage

Juvenal's evocative phrase for any story we have been subjected to time after time after time, and for any literary work made stale by repetition. While *crambe repetita* is well translated as "stale repetitions," the word *crambe* alone is literally translated as "cabbage," and everyone who knows cabbage realizes that it stinks after it has been cooked too long.

cras credemus, hodie nihil
krahs KRAY-deh-muus HAW-dee-ay NIH-hil
tomorrow we'll believe, today not

> Often interpreted as "small minds are closed to new ideas."

cras mihi
krahs MIH-hih
my turn tomorrow

> The motto of any younger sibling. After all, fair is fair. A related phrase, but not as generous, is **hodie mihi, cras tibi** (HAW-dee-ay MIH-hih krahs TIH-bih), "my turn today, yours tomorrow."

crassa negligentia
KRAHS-sah neh-glih-GEN-tee-ah
gross negligence

> A legal term implying culpability for the perpetrator of the act so characterized.

crede experto
KRAY-day ek-SPEHR-toh
believe the experienced person

> Also given as EXPERTO CREDE, with the same meaning. It must be understood that we are not being advised to believe an expert. Today's experts too often turn out to be little more than persons paid to agree with the person who hires them. The adjective *expertus* (eks-PEHR-tuus) and its inflected forms mean "experienced."

crede quod habes, et habes
KRAY-day kwawd HAH-behs et HAH-behs
think positively

A plug for self-confidence, literally "believe that you have it, and you have it."

crede ut intelligas
KRAY-day uut in-TEL-lih-gahs
believe so that you may understand

This injunction is directed at those who seek a basis for their faith or the faith they seek, implying that faith does not begin with understanding, but ends in understanding.

credite posteri
KRAY-dih-tay PAWS-teh-ree
you'd better believe it!

Horace exhorting future generations to believe what he has written. His message translates literally as "let posterity believe it." A memoirist would do well to write *credite posteri* at the head of an opening chapter.

credula res amor est
KRAY-duu-lah rays AH-mawr est
people in love will believe anything

Ovid, a keen observer, telling us "a credulous thing is love." So what else is new?

crescit amor nummi quantum ipsa pecunia crescit
KRAY-skit AH-mawr NUUM-mee KWAHN-tuum IH-psah peh-KOO-nee-ah KRAY-skit
the more you have, the more you want

Juvenal's dismal observation, literally "the love of money grows as wealth increases," makes it clear that avarice has been with us at least since the time of ancient Rome, and there's no containing it. How else to explain the modern phenomenon of rapidly growing wealth of the already wealthy while more and more people sink deeper into poverty?

crescit sub pondere virtus
KRAY-skit suub PAWN-deh-reh WIHR-toos
virtue grows under oppression

Adversity often brings out the best in people.

cribro aquam haurire
KREE-broh AH-kwahm how-REE-reh
to draw water in a sieve

A hopeless pursuit. Don't waste your time in unproductive effort.

crimen falsi
KREE-men FAHL-see
the crime of forgery

This phrase may also be translated as "the crime of falsehood."

crimen laesae maiestatis
KREE-men LĪ-sī mī-eh-STAH-tihs
high treason

A legal term denoting what was formerly called the crime of lese majesty, an offense against the dignity of a ruler. Back when kings were kings, this was a matter of utmost seriousness. Today, with kings usually out of the picture, any high treason is directed against the state.

crux
kruuks

cross

The word *crux* has several meanings in addition to "cross." For example, it can be translated as "gallows," "perplexing problem," "puzzle," or "torment" and appears in several phrases: **crux criticorum** (krih-tih-KOH-ruum, "of critics");

crux interpretum (in-TEHR-preh-tuum, "of translators or interpreters"); **crux mathematicorum** (mah-tay-mah-tih-KOH-ruum, "of mathematicians"); and **crux medicorum** (meh-dih-KOH-ruum, "of physicians"). Any of the five meanings supplied here for *crux* may be used in interpreting these phrases.

cucullus non facit monachum
kuu-KUUL-luus nohn FAH-kit maw-NAH-kuum
the cowl does not make the monk

This proverb tells us not to be deceived by mere trappings. And just as it takes more than a change of uniform to make a basketball superstar a journeyman major league baseball player, more than a vow to transform a sinner, and more than a caning or thrashing to reform a felon, it takes more than a stern lecture to teach a child manners. (For a contrary opinion, see VESTIS VIRUM FACIT.)

cui peccare licet, peccat minus
KOO-ee pek-KAH-reh LEE-ket PEK-kaht MEE-nuus
he who is free to sin, sins less

Wise words from Ovid.

cuique suum
KOO-ee-kweh SOO-uum
to each his own

cuius est divisio, alterius est electio
KOO-yuus est dih-WEE-see-oh ahl-teh-REE-uus est ay-LAY-ktee-oh
one cuts the pie, the other has the first slice

Very practical advice is given here, literally "whichever (of two parties) makes the division, the other makes the choice." When a partnership—a marriage, for example—must be dissolved, disagreement is almost certain to arise over how to split assets held in common. So one party divides the assets, and the other chooses the half he or she desires. Wisdom rivaling Solomon's.

culpae poena par esto
KUUL-pī POY-nah pahr EH-stoh
let the punishment be proportioned to the crime

This principle has long been considered a cornerstone of criminal justice. One problem with this principle lies in the changing mood of the public, so what once appeared to be appropriate punishment for a given crime may now appear too lenient or too harsh. Nevertheless, recall W.S. Gilbert's lines from *The Mikado:*

> My object all sublime
> I shall achieve in time—
> To make the punishment fit the crime.

(See also NOXIAE POENA PAR ESTO.)

culpa lata
KUUL-pah LAH-tah
gross neglect

A term in law, as opposed to **culpa levis** (LEH-wihs), "excusable neglect."

culpam maiorum posteri luunt
KUUL-pahm mah-YAWR-uum PAWS-teh-ree LOO-uunt
the sins of the fathers

A sobering observation, literally "descendants pay for the shortcomings of their ancestors." What we say and do may affect future generations. (See also VIVIMUS IN POSTERIS.)

culpam poena premit comes
KUUL-pahm POY-nah PREH-mit KAW-mehs
punishment presses hard upon the heels of crime

Horace warning anyone contemplating commission of a crime that crime does not pay. Modern criminals don't read Horace.

cum bona venia
kuum BAW-nah WAY-nee-ah
with your kind indulgence

cum multis aliis
kuum MUUL-tees AH-lih-ees
with many others

cum permissu superiorum
kuum pehr-MEES-soo suu-peh-ree-OH-ruum
with the permission of superiors

cuneus cuneum trudit
KUU-neh-uus KUU-neh-uum TROO-dit
steady effort pays off

The literal meaning of *cuneus cuneum trudit* is "wedge drives wedge." And just as a small opening made by a thin wedge can by persistent effort with additional wedges bring down the largest tree, small beginnings of any kind can eventually lead to great achievement—or to disaster.

currus bovem trahit
KUUR-ruus BOH-wem TRAH-hit
don't put the cart before the horse

It's a mistake to deal with minor matters before getting down to the central issue confronting you, as we are warned in *currus bovem trahit*, literally "the wagon drags the ox." In planning any activity, we must keep first things first.

curta supellex
KUUR-tah suu-PEL-leks
a meager store of knowledge

The literal meaning of this phrase, "a scanty supply of furniture," provides an interesting characterization of someone who knows little. Now we have a substitute for the tired phrase "no rocket scientist."

D

da dextrum misero
dah DEH-kstruum MIH-seh-roh
extend a hand to the needy

In a time when men and women live on the streets of the self-styled richest nation on earth, this injunction of Virgil, literally "give a right hand to the wretched," is surely appropriate. (See also DATE OBOLUM BELISARIO.)

da locum melioribus
dah LAW-kuum meh-lee-OH-rih-buus
give way to your betters

Terence asking for respect for superiors.

dante Deo
DAHN-teh DAY-oh
by the gift of God

dapes inemptae
DAH-pehs in-EM-ptī
homegrown food

A friendly phrase, literally "feasts unbought," useful for health devotees, fans of organically grown foodstuffs, and protectors of the natural environment—the most assiduous of whom grow their own food for the table.

dare fatis vela
DAH-reh FAH-tihs WAY-lah
to sail where fate directs

Virgil's advice to sailors—and others making their way through life—literally "to give the sails to the fates." Things will probably turn out right. (See also DATA FATA SECUTUS.)

dare pondus idonea fumo
DAH-reh PAWN-duus ih-DOH-neh-ah FOO-moh
absolutely worthless

Persius offering book critics a damning phrase sure not to be quoted in advertisements, literally "fit only to give weight to smoke." Unfortunately, *dare pondus idonea fumo* may evoke images of book burning. Perhaps it is better to say "useful only as a doorstop."

data fata secutus
DAH-tah FAH-tah seh-KOO-tuus
following what fate decrees

Virgil, Roman to the core, recognizing the power of ineluctable destiny. (See also DARE FATA VELIS.)

date obolum Belisario
DAH-tay OH-boh-luum beh-lih-SAH-ree-oh
give alms to a beggar

Belisarius, a great general serving Roman emperor Justinian (6th century A.D.), was accused of conspiracy to overthrow Justinian and was imprisoned for a few months. It is said unreliably that his captors put his eyes out and Belisarius was reduced to begging. Belisarius is remembered in *date obolum Belisario*, literally "give a penny to Belisarius." An obolus is a

modern Greek coin of little value. (See also DA DEXTRUM MIS-
ERO.)

Davus sum, non Oedipus
DAH-wuus suum nohn OY-dih-poos
I'm just an average Joe, not an eye surgeon

This line from Terence, literally "I am Davus, not Oedipus,"
can be freely translated as "I am an ordinary man, and no
solver of riddles like Oedipus." Davus may be thought of as
Everyman, while Oedipus, it will be recalled, solved the riddle
of the Sphinx:

> What goes on four feet, on two feet, and three,
> But the more feet it goes on the weaker it be?

Oedipus solved the riddle, answering that it was a man: as
an infant, he crawls on all fours, in manhood walks erect on
two feet, and in old age requires a cane to support his legs.

dea certe
DEH-ah KEHR-tay
assuredly a goddess

A fine compliment to pay any woman of outstanding
achievement in her lifetime.

de alieno corio liberalis
day ah-lee-AY-noh KAW-ree-oh lee-beh-RAH-lihs
free with other people's money

Literally "generous with another person's leather."

de auditu
day ow-DEE-too
by hearing *or* hearsay

debellare superbos
day-bel-LAH-reh SUU-pehr-baws
to subdue the arrogant

debemur morti nos nostraque
DAY-beh-muur MAWR-tee nohs NAW-strah-kweh
we are destined for death, we and our works

    Horace had almost all of this right, but his own works destined for death? Not a chance. (See also DEFICIT OMNE QUOD NASCITUR.)

debitum naturae
DAY-bih-tuum nah-TOO-rī
the debt to nature

    A euphemism for "death" and evocative of "ashes to ashes and dust to dust" in suggesting that all of us are merely on loan to the world.

de bonis propriis
day BAW-nees PRAW-prih-ees
out of his own pocket

    Literally "from his own goods."

decessit sine prole
day-KEHS-sit SIH-neh PROH-leh
he or she died without issue

    Childless, that is.

decet imperatorem stantem mori
DEH-ket ihm-peh-rah-TOH-rem STAHN-tem MAWR-ee
it is fitting that an emperor die standing

    Said to be the dying words of the Roman emperor Vespasian (1st century A.D.), who is reported to have stood upright while awaiting his death. It is also reported that the upright English queen Elizabeth I (1533–1603) died upright.

decies repetita placebit
DEH-kee-ays reh-peh-TEE-tah PLAH-keh-bit
some things are worth hearing over and over again

Literally "though ten times repeated, it will continue to please." Horace tells us that works of quality—poems, plays, or musical compositions—will never pall. He was not alluding to the stale stories told again and again by husbands and other bores.

decipit frons prima multos
day-KIH-pit frohns PREE-mah MUUL-tohs
beware of first impressions

Wise words from Horace, "the first appearance deceives many," cautioning young people and old fools against precipitate judgments of people they meet—in particular warning against falling in love too fast.

decumanus fluctus
deh-kuu-MAH-nuus FLOOK-tuus
the Big One

Literally "the tenth wave." An ominous phrase reflecting the ancient and persistent notion that the tenth wave in a recurring natural movement—for example, tidal action or seismic activity—is thought to be by far the largest or most powerful. And Californians pay heed to the Richter scale and count shocks and aftershocks, waiting for the ninth, tenth, eleventh. . .

de dolo malo
day DAW-loh MAH-loh
from evil intent

A legal term, also translated as "from willful fraud."

deficit omne quod nascitur
day-FIH-kit AWM-neh kwawd NAH-skee-tuur
nothing is certain but death and taxes

Quintilian calling attention, in case anyone forgets, to the transitory nature of life, literally "everything that is born passes away." It is Benjamin Franklin who is credited with first calling attention to the inevitability of death and taxes. (See also DEBEMUR MORTI NON NOSTRAQUE.)

de fumo in flammam
day FOO-moh in FLAHM-mahm
out of the frying pan into the fire

Surely the English phrase given above, which dates from the 16th century, is more striking than its Latin progenitor, literally "out of the smoke into the flame." Whichever you prefer, take care that in trying to get out of a sticky situation you do not immediately fall into a worse one.

degeneres animos timor arguit
day-GEN-eh-rehs AH-nih-mohs TIH-mawr AHR-goo-eet
fear betrays base souls

Virgil's judgment of cowards.

de gratia
day GRAH-tee-ah
from favor *or* by favor

When we do anything *de gratia*, we do it "willingly," out of the goodness of our hearts.

Dei sub numine viget
DEH-ee suub NOO-mih-neh WIH-get
it flourishes under the will of God

Motto of Princeton University.

deiecta (or dejecta) arbore quivis ligna colligit
day-YEH-ktah AHR-bawr-eh KWEE-wihs LIH-gnah
KAWL-lih-git
standing by while others struggle

This proverb, literally "when the tree is felled, anyone gathers the wood," tells us that lazy people too often profit from the hard work of others.

de lana caprina
day LAH-nah kah-PREE-nah
about anything worthless

A phrase adapted from Horace, literally "about goat's wool," used to characterize a worthless discussion or other unproductive activity. Goat's wool is suggestive of worthlessness because goats have hair, not wool. So we may say, "They foolishly spend their time talking *de lana caprina.*" It is interesting to note that *caprina* may also be translated as "underarm odor." (See also RIXATUR DE LANA SAEPE CAPRINA.)

deliberando saepe perit occasio
day-lee-beh-RAHN-doh SĪ-peh PEHR-eet awk-KAH-see-
oh
let's get down to business

One of the worst things we can do when we are considering a problem that's crying out for solution is discuss and discuss interminably. Publilius Syrus, here giving us yet another of his compelling observations, tells us literally that "opportunity is often lost by considering too long."

delphinum natare doces
del-FEE-nuum nah-TAH-reh DOH-kehs
you're teaching a dolphin how to swim

This rebuke means "you are teaching an experienced person how to do something he already knows how to do." Primarily among the British, this thought is conveyed idiomatically in "you're teaching your grandmother [how] to suck eggs." (See also AQUILAM VOLARE DOCES.)

denique caelum
DAY-nih-kweh KĪ-luum
heaven at last!

Battle cry of the Crusaders of the late Middle Ages.

deorum cibus est
deh-OH-ruum KIH-buus est
it is food for the gods

destitutis ventis remos adhibe
day-stih-TOO-tihs WEN-tees RAY-mohs ahd-HIH-beh
try anything, it may work

When disaster threatens, Americans are apt to say, "Don't just sit there. Do something." The Romans had the same thought, expressed literally here as "when the winds fail, take to the oars."

desunt inopiae multa, avaritiae omnia
DAY-suunt in-AW-pee-ī MUUL-tah ah-wah-RIH-tih-ī AWM-nee-ah
poverty wants many things, avarice wants everything

Publilius Syrus saying it all about greed.

desunt multa
DAY-suunt MUUL-tah
many things are wanting

detur digniore
DAY-tuur dih-gnih-OH-reh
let it be given to one more worthy

The Latin appropriate for the rare situation in which one turns down a proffered award.

Deus avertat!
DEH-uus ah-WEHR-taht
God forbid!

dextras dare
DEHK-strahs DAH-reh
shake on it

Literally "to give right hands"; more freely, "to shake hands as a pledge of mutual trust."

dextro tempore
DEHK-stroh TEM-paw-reh
at a favorable *or* lucky moment

The Romans scarcely made a move without consulting a seer, who would tell them whether the time was right for a contemplated action—usually in ambiguous language protective of the seer's reputation for giving reliable advice.

dicamus bona verba
DEE-kah-muus BAW-nah WEHR-bah
let us speak words of good omen

Literally "let us speak good words."

dicta docta pro datis
DIH-ktah DAW-ktah proh DAH-tihs
words are cheap

A thought from Plautus, "clever speeches in place of giving gifts."

dictum ac factum
DIH-ktuum ahk FAH-ktuum
no sooner said than done

> Literally "said and done."

dictum de dicto
DIH-ktuum day DIH-ktoh
a hearsay report

> Literally "a saying from a saying."

dictum sapienti sat est
DIH-ktuum sah-pee-EN-tih saht est
a word to the wise is sufficient

> A proverb attributed to Plautus.

difficilia quae pulchra
dif-fih-KIH-lee-ah kwī PUUL-krah
beautiful things are difficult

> To achieve, that is.

digito monstrari
DIH-gih-toh mohn-STRAH-ree
to be a celebrity

> Plautus indicating, literally "to be pointed out with the finger," the recognition accorded a famous person.

dii minores
DEE-ee mih-NOH-rehs
men of second rank

> Literally "lesser gods."

dii pia facta vident
DEE-ee PEE-ah FAH-ktah WIH-dent
someone is watching

Ovid telling us literally in "the gods see upright deeds" that whatever good we do will not go unrecognized.

dimidium facti qui coepit habet
dee-MIH-dih-uum FAH-ktee kwee KOY-pit HAH-bet
advice for procrastinators

Horace urging us to get started, literally "he who makes a start has half the work done."

diminuere Priscianis caput
dih-mih-NOO-eh-reh pree-skee-AH-nihs KAH-puut
to violate rules of grammar

Priscian was a 6th-century A.D. grammarian at Constantinople whose textbook of Latin grammar was used widely. He is remembered today for *diminuere Priscianis caput*, literally "to make Priscian's head smaller," and in its usual English rendering, "to break Priscian's head." Both mean "to be guilty of solecisms."

divitiae virum faciunt
dee-WIH-tee-ī WIHR-uum FAH-kee-uunt
riches make the man

A cynical, but in many circles realistic, view of the world.

domat omnia virtus
DAW-maht AWM-nee-ah WIHR-tuus
virtue conquers all things

The Romans made much of virtue, as you surely realize by now. If, by chance, you have not seen *virtus* until now, turn to the several entries that begin with this word. (By way of contrast, see also DIVITIAE VIRUM FACIUNT.)

domus et placens uxor
DAW-muus et PLAH-kens UU-ksawr
home and a satisfying wife

Horace speaking of all a man needs to be happy. But what does a woman need? Horace is silent.

domus sua cuique est tutissimum refugium
DAW-muus SOO-ah KOO-ee-kweh est tuu-TIHS-sih-muum reh-FUU-gee-uum
every man's home is his safest refuge

In an English version of this proverb going back about four centuries, "a man's house is his castle."

duabus sellis sedere
doo-AH-buus SEHL-lihs seh-DAY-reh
to take both sides in a dispute

This metaphor may be translated more literally as "to be seated in two seats" or much less than literally as "to wear two hats."

duas tantum res anxius optat, panem et circenses
DOO-ahs TAHN-tuum rays AHN-ksih-uus AW-ptaht PAH-nem et keer-KAYN-says
keep the masses fed and entertained

According to Juvenal, the cynical formula for ruling the Roman populace successfully, which may be translated as "two things only do the people earnestly desire, bread and circus games."

ducunt volentem fata, nolentum trahunt
DOO-kuunt waw-LAYN-tem FAH-tah noh-LEN-tuum
TRAH-huunt
the fates lead the willing, drag the unwilling

Seneca on the inevitability of destiny—no matter whether
we resist or not, the outcome is the same.

dulce bellum inexpertis
DUUL-kĕh BEL-luum in-ek-SPEHR-tihs
only people who have never served advocate war

A realistic—but surely incorrect—observation, translated
nearly literally as "sweet is war to those who have never tried
it."

dulce quod utile
DUUL-keh kwawd OO-tih-leh
pleasant is that which is useful

dulcis amor patriae
DUUL-kihs AH-mawr PAH-trih-ī
sweet is the love of one's native land

dum loquor, hora fugit
duum LOH-kwawr HOH-rah FUU-git
no more talking if I'm to get anything done

Ovid, who knew he had better things to do with his time,
saying "time is flying while I speak." (See also AMICI FURES TEM-
PORES.)

dummodo sit dives, barbarus ipse placet
DUUM-maw-daw sit DEE-wehs BAHR-bahr-uus IH-pseh
PLAH-ket
when money talks, everybody listens

Ovid telling us that people are always willing to put up with anybody who is wealthy, literally "so long as he is rich, even a barbarian is pleasing."

dum vitant stulti vitia in contraria current
duum WEE-tahnt STUUL-tih WIH-tih-ah in kawn-TRAH-ree-ah KUUR-rent
in shunning vices, fools run to opposite extremes

Horace telling us to use moderation when attempting to improve our own behavior. One step at a time is better than cold turkey.

duos qui sequitur lepores neutrum capit
DOO-aws kwee SEH-kwih-tuur leh-POH-rehs neh-HEHOO-truum KAH-pit
he who chases two hares catches neither one

One bullet cannot hit two targets.

E

e consensu gentium
ay kohn-SAYN-soo GEN-tee-uum
out of general agreement of mankind

An argument based on general agreement of reasonable people is an *argumentum* (ahr-goo-MEN-tuum) *e consensu gentium*.

edax rerum
EH-dahks RAY-ruum
gluttonous

Literally "devouring of things," describing the proclivity of voracious eaters. (See also EDO ERGO SUM.) Ovid applied *edax rerum* to time in *tempus* (TEM-puus) *edax rerum*, usually translated as "time, the devourer of all things."

edo ergo sum

EH-doh EHR-goh suum

I eat, therefore I exist

A sure sign of vitality, since dead men don't eat. *Edo ergo sum* is evocative of the famous axiom of Descartes, **cogito ergo sum** (KOH-gih-toh EHR-goh suum), "I think, therefore I exist."

e flamma petere cibum

ay FLAHM-mah PEH-teh-reh KIH-buum

to live by desperate means

A phrase of Terence, literally "to seek food out of the flame," suggesting the mind-set of people on their uppers who are willing to face any danger in order to survive.

ego spem pretio non emo

EH-goh spem PREH-tee-oh nohn EH-moh

show me

Where we might say, "I don't buy a pig in a poke," Terence said, "I don't purchase hope for a price."

eiusdem generis

AY-uus-dem GEH-neh-rihs

of the same kind

The same meaning is conveyed by **eiusdem farinae**, literally "of the same flour." One might describe two criminals, for example, as *eiusdem generis* or *eiusdem farinae*.

eius nulla culpa est cui parere necesse sit

AY-uus NUUL-lah KUUL-pah est KOO-ee pah-RAY-reh neh-KES-seh sit

a man forced to obey is not at fault for what he does

This axiom suggests we go slow in judging anyone who

acts under duress. Consider what you and I might do under similar circumstances.

elapso tempore
eh-LAH-psoh TEM-paw-reh
the time having elapsed

elephantem ex musca facis
eh-leh-FAHN-tuum eks MUU-skah FAH-kihs
you're making a mountain out of a molehill

Literally "you're making an elephant out of a fly."

elephantus non capit murem
eh-leh-FAHN-tuus nohn KAH-pit MOO-rem
an elephant does not capture a mouse

This saying, translated literally above, can be taken to mean "important people don't occupy themselves with trifles." It can also mean "be sure to use an appropriate tool (or punishment) to achieve the purpose you have in mind."

empta dolore docet experientia
EM-ptah daw-LOH-reh DAW-ket eks-peh-rih-EN-tee-ah
a once-burnt child shuns fire from then on

More literally "experience bought with pain teaches effectively."

e multis paleis paulam fructus collegi
ay MUUL-tees PAH-leh-ihs POW-lahm FRUUK-tuus kawl-LEH-gee
a few pearls of wisdom scattered in a desert of words

This observation, literally "from much chaff I have gathered a little grain," expresses the disappointment we often feel after wading through a tedious book or article and finding only a few worthwhile thoughts.

emunctae naris
ay-MUUN-ktī NAH-rihs
of mature judgment

Horace, in characterizing a person of keen judgment or perception, hit it right on the nose with *emunctae naris*, literally "of cleared nostril" or "with blown nose." Anyone qualified to judge—not only sniff—the quality of something put before him can be expected to offer a sound appraisal. (See also SUSPENDENS OMNIA NASO for another nasal metaphor from Horace.)

Epicuri de grege porcus
eh-pih-KOO-ree day GREH-geh PAWR-kuus
a glutton

Horace's phrase, "a hog from the drove of Epicurus." Epicurus (341-270 B.C.), a Greek philosopher and moral theorist, was given a bum rap when his moral theory—seeking the minimization of pain by avoidance of unnecessary fears and desires—which we call Epicureanism, began to be perceived in the popular mind as advocating riotous living and indulgence of the appetites. Thus the meaning "a glutton" given above.

epistola non erubescit
eh-PIHS-taw-lah nohn ay-ruu-BAY-skit
easier to put it in writing

We can put things in letters—for example, expressions of admiration, love, rejection, or hatred—that we may find difficult to say directly to someone. Thus Cicero's advice, literally "a letter does not blush," on the advantages of writing letters.

equi frenato est auris in ore
EH-kwee fray-NAH-toh est OW-rihs in OH-reh
what to do when someone won't listen

When words are not heeded, a show of force may be needed to get someone's attention. As Horace put it in this adage, literally "the ear of a horse is in its bridled mouth," the only recourse may be to inflict some pain. Thus, it is not always worthwhile to constantly forgive and forget.

e re nata
ay ray NAH-tah
as matters stand

A useful phrase, also interpreted as "under the circumstances" and "as things are."

ergo bibamus!
EHR-goh bih-BAH-muus
let's break out a bottle!

A call for merrymaking, literally "therefore, let us drink," that may go out when a big project—for example, the tedious copying of a text by a monk—is finally completed. Also expressed as **nunc est bibendum** (nuunk est bih-BEN-duum), "now it is time to drink."

eripuit caelo fulmen sceptrumque tyrannis
ay-RIH-poo-eet KĪ-loh FUUL-men SKAY-ptruum-kweh tih-RAHN-nihs
he snatched the thunderbolt from heaven and the scepter from tyrants

The legend, adapted from Manilius, inscribed under the bust of Benjamin Franklin—our famous diplomat and kite-flier—that was sculpted by Jean-Antoine Houdon (1741-1828).

est ars etiam male dicendi
est ahrs EH-tee-ahm MAH-leh dee-KEN-dee
there's an art even to speaking evil

Advice to the heavy-handed derogator.

est deus in nobis
est DEH-uus in NOH-bihs
there is a god within us

Ovid reminding us that good and the capability to do worthwhile things reside in all of us.

esto quod esse videris
EH-stoh kwawd ES-seh wih-DAY-rihs
be what you seem to be

Avoiding pretense makes life easier all around.

est quaedam flere voluptas
est KWĪ-dahm FLAY-reh waw-LUU-ptahs
there is a certain pleasure in weeping

Insight from Ovid.

estque pati poenas quam meruisse minus
EST-kweh PAH-tee POY-nahs kwahm meh-roo-EES-seh MIH-nuus
it's better to suffer punishment than to deserve it

Ovid telling us to face the music instead of living in dread.

esurienti ne occurras
ay-suur-ee-AYN-tee nay awk-KUUR-rahs
don't take on an impoverished opponent

This maxim, literally "don't attack a hungry person," cautions us that even the weak may become dangerous when impelled by severe privation.

et alibi
et AH-lih-bee
and elsewhere

This phrase—like **et alii** (AHL-lee-ee, "and other men"), **et aliae** (AH-lee-ī, "and other women"), and **et alia** (AH-lee-ah, "and other things")—is abbreviated **et al**.

et ego in Arcadia
et EH-goh in ahr-KAH-dee-ah
I have known true contentment

Arcadia, a region of southern Greece, epitomized rural happiness, so this statement, literally "I too have been in Arcadia," can be read to indicate contentment with one's past life. Yet, when used as a tombstone inscription, it can be read as "I (Death) am even in Arcadia," indicating that death is everywhere. As though we didn't already know it.

et genus et formam regina pecunia donat
et GEN-uus et FAWR-mahm RAY-gee-nah peh-KOO-nee-ah DOH-naht
is there anything money can't buy?

A realistic, albeit cynical, observation of Horace, literally "money, like a queen, gives both rank and beauty." At least in the eyes of some. (See also NON DEFICIENTE CRUMENA.)

etiam capillus unus habet umbram suam
EH-tee-ahm kah-PIL-luus OON-uus HAH-bet UUM-brahm SOO-ahm
don't take anyone or anything for granted

Publilius Syrus telling us, in "even a single hair has its shadow," that we must give due attention to everyone and everything in our lives, no matter how apparently insignificant.

etiam perire ruinae
EH-tee-ahm peh-REE-reh ruu-EEN-ī
even the ruins have perished

A sad observation of Lucan, telling us humanity's past glories have disappeared. And the Romans did their part in destroying them.

etiam sanato vulnere cicatrix manet
EH-tee-ahm sah-NAH-toh WUUL-neh-reh KIH-kah-treeks MAH-net
even when the wound has healed, the scar remains

And we never forget the wound—with or without professional assistance. (See also CICATRIX MANET.)

etiam si Cato dicat
EH-tee-ahm see KAH-toh DEE-kaht
even if Cato were to say it

Cato was a man of strict justice and blunt speech, so to his contemporaries anything he said was taken as true. The phrase *etiam si Cato dicat*, therefore, is used to express incredulity, as in "I wouldn't believe what you are telling me *etiam si Cato dicat.*"

etiam stultis acuit ingenuit fames
EH-tee-ahm STUUL-tihs AH-koo-eet in-GEH-noo-eet FAH-mays
a potent motivator

This proverb, "hunger sharpens the wits even of fools," tells us that when hunger strikes, even dullards become resourceful. And when they do, who knows what desperate actions may ensue?

et modo quae fuerat semita facta via est
et MAW-daw kwī FOO-eh-raht SAY-mee-tah FAH-ktah WEE-ah est
next come the shopping malls

Martial, in writing that "and what had been only a footpath became a highway," looked happily on the changes wrought by advancing civilization. He never envisioned how things would turn out in the next millennia.

et qui nolunt occidere quemquam posse volunt
et kwee NOH-luunt awk-KIH-deh-reh KWEM-kwahm PAWS-seh WOH-luunt
is this why crime stories dominate prime time?

Juvenal, observing the dark side of human nature, wrote "those who do not wish to kill anyone wish they were able."

et sceleratis sol oritur
et skeh-leh-RAH-tihs sohl AWR-ih-tuur
the sun shines even on the wicked

Seneca, providing the original model for a 16th-century English proverb, "the sun shines on all alike," meaning that nature treats all people the same or, in a modern interpretation, all men are created equal. What happens once the level playing field has had its chance is anyone's guess and the responsibility of each of us.

et semel emissum volat irrevocabile verbum
et SEH-mel ay-MIHS-suum WOH-laht ihr-reh-woh-KAH-bih-leh WEHR-buum
watch what you say

Horace, who understood how nasty words can have consequences, cautioning us to be circumspect in our speech, literally "and a word once uttered flies away, never to be recalled."

eventus stultorum magister
ay-WEHN-tuus stuul-TAWR-uum mah-GIH-stehr
fools can only learn through experience

Livy, telling us literally that "the result is the instructor of fools" and, by implication, there is no other way for fools to learn. (See also EMPTA DOLORE DOCET EXPERIENTIA, which makes a similar comment on how children learn.)

e vestigio
ay wehs-TEE-gih-oh
instantly

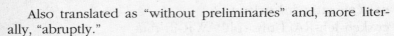

ex abrupto
eks ah-BRUU-ptaw
out of the blue

Also translated as "without preliminaries" and, more literally, "abruptly."

ex abundante cautela
eks ah-buun-DAHN-teh kow-TAY-lah
from excessive caution

Excessive caution can paralyze.

ex Africa semper aliquid novi
eks AH-frih-kah SEM-pehr AH-lih-kwid NAW-wee
there is always something new out of Africa

This saying, an allusion to the ancient belief that Africa abounded in strange monsters, derives from a Greek proverb quoted by Pliny the Elder. Incidentally, to the ancients, Africa was a Roman province, now called Tunisia.

ex arena funiculum nectis
eks ah-RAY-nah foo-NIH-kuu-luum NEH-ktihs
you're attempting the impossible

Literally "you're weaving a rope of sand." (See also ARENAE MANDAS SEMINA and ARENA SINE CALCE.)

exceptis excipiendis
eks-KEH-ptees eks-kih-pee-EN-dees
due exceptions being made

In generalizations we make, that is.

excerpta
eks-KEHR-ptah
excerpts

Also translated as "extracts" and "selections."

ex commodo
eks KAWM-maw-doh
conveniently *or* at one's convenience

ex confesso
eks kohn-FEH-soh
admittedly *or* confessedly

ex desuetudina amittuntur privilegia
eks day-soo-ay-TOO-dih-nah ah-mit-TUUN-tuur pree-
wih-LAY-gee-ah
use it or lose it

A legal maxim, "by disuse are privileges lost."

exempla sunt odiosa
ek-SEM-plah suunt aw-dih-OH-sah
examples are odious

We are accustomed to hearing the 15th-century proverb
"comparisons are odious," meaning that the drawing of analo-
gies is offensive. Now we find as well that examples must be
chosen with great care lest they also be seen as offensive.

exemplo plus quam ratione vivimus
ek-SEM-ploh ploos kwahm rah-tih-OH-neh WEE-wih-muus

do what I do, not what I say

A maxim, literally "we live more by example than by reason," suggesting that we are influenced less by moral precepts—taught usually by teachers, parents, or ministers—than by what we see these same people do.

ex eodem ore calidum et frigidum efflare
eks eh-OH-dem OH-reh KAH-lih-duum et FREE-gih-duum ehf-FLAH-reh

to blow hot and cold from the same mouth

To give conflicting signals—a confusing and discouraging type of behavior.

exercitatio optimus est magister
eks-ehr-kih-TAH-tee-oh AW-ptih-muus est mah-GIH-stehr

practice is the best instructor

Or, as we are wont to say, practice makes perfect.

ex fide fortis
eks FIH-day FAWR-tihs

strong through faith

ex granis fit acervus
eks GRAHN-ees feet ah-KEHR-wuus

Keogh plans plus IRAs—every bit helps

We all know—and who would deny?—that assiduity pays off in the end. The problem is that too many of us are unhappy with anything but an immediate payoff. The rest act in accordance with this proverb, literally "many grains make a heap," and put aside a little out of each paycheck. Sure

enough, the savers do achieve financial independence in their
retirement years—with the help of Social Security, that is.

ex imo corde
eks EE-moh KAWR-deh
from the bottom of the heart

ex improviso
eks ihm-proh-WEE-soh
suddenly *or* unexpectedly

ex natura rerum
eks nah-TOO-rah RAY-ruum
from the nature of things

ex necessitate
eks neh-kehs-sih-TAH-teh
from necessity *or* necessarily

ex ore parvulorum veritas
eks OH-reh pahr-wuu-LOH-ruum WAY-rih-tahs
out of the mouths of babes (comes) truth

So we should always listen to what children say.

ex oriente lux, ex occidente lex
eks aw-rih-AYN-teh luuks eks awk-kih-DEN-teh layks
enlightenment from the East, our practical side from the
West

Devotees of Eastern philosophy and religion will probably
prefer the free rendering of *ex oriente lux, ex occidente lex*
given above rather than its literal translation, "light (comes)
out of the East, law from the West."

experientia docet
eks-peh-ree-EHN-tee-ah DAW-ket
we learn from experience

Literally "experience teaches." (See also USUS EST OPTIMUS MAGISTER and USUS TE PLURA DOCEBIT.)

experto crede

See CREDE EXPERTO.

expertus metuit
eks-PEHR-tuus MEH-tuu-eet
the experienced man is apprehensive

In propounding this wisdom, Horace had in mind the dangers inherent in cultivating the friendship of powerful people—be careful lest you get burned! So Horace is telling us that while we may think it wonderful to rub shoulders with the politically powerful, people who have been around the track a few times are always on guard and take pains to protect themselves.

explorant adversa viros
eks-PLOH-rahnt ahd-WEHR-sah WIHR-aws
when the going gets tough, the tough get going

Literally "misfortunes put men to the test."

expressis verbis
eks-PREHS-sees WEHR-bees
in so many words

Literally "in explicit terms."

ex scintilla incendium
eks skin-TIHL-lah in-KEN-dih-uum
from a spark a conflagration

A minor problem uncorrected can build and build and finally end in catastrophe—a two-bit break-in can eventually bring down a U.S. president. Going back a few centuries, we have the English proverb "for want of a nail the shoe is lost, for want of a shoe the horse is lost, for want of a horse the rider is lost."

ex umbra in solem
eks UUM-brah in SOH-lem
from shade into sunlight

Our so-called sunshine laws exemplify *ex umbra in solem*, casting light on official government records and meetings by granting access previously denied to the public. (See also QUI MALE AGIT ODIT LUCEM.)

ex umbris et imaginibus in veritatem
eks UUM-brihs et ih-mah-GIH-nih-buus in way-rih-TAH-tem
from shadows and apparitions to reality

This was the epitaph of Cardinal Newman (1801-1891), alluding to the soul's journey to God. (See COR AD COR LOQUITUR for his motto.)

ex vitio alterius sapiens emendat suum
eks WIH-tee-oh ahl-TAY-ree-uus SAH-pih-ayns ay-MEN-daht SOO-uum
learn from the mistakes of others

Publilius Syrus, telling us literally—and hopefully—"from another's fault, a wise person corrects his own." (See also EVENTUS STULTORUM MAGISTER, which tells us that fools do not learn anything from the mistakes of others.)

ex vitulo bos fit
eks WIH-tuu-loh bohs feet
from a calf comes an ox

And not a giraffe or a crocodile. Thus, when we raise a child to be self-reliant, the child does not become a clinging vine, and when we habitually abuse a child, the child grows up to be an abuser of children. Or so we are told.

F

faber est quisque fortunae suae
FAH-behr est KWIS-kweh fawr-TOO-nī SOO-ī
everyone is the architect of his own success

Or failure, since *fortunae suae* can also be translated as "his own misfortune."

fac et excusa
fahk et ek-SKOO-sah
make your move

Fac et excusa, which can stand as the motto of successful people—all of whom have surely had their shares of mistakes and failures—translates literally as "do it and make excuses later." The worst thing one can do is habitually put off and put off and put off, whether because of uncertainty about the correctness of planned actions or because penalties for possible errors look too onerous.

facies tua computat annos
FAH-kee-ays TOO-ah kawm-POO-taht AHN-nohs
check the mirror, not the calendar

Juvenal telling all of us literally "your face keeps count of the years." Of course, today we have sunblock and plastic surgery for those who do not appreciate what they may see in their mirrors.

facile est inventis addere
FAH-kih-leh est in-WEN-tihs AHD-deh-reh
that's why editors were born

Literally "it's easy to add to things already invented." And, of course, it's hard to do anything original.

facile largiri de alieno
FAH-kih-leh lahr-GEE-ree day ah-lee-AY-noh
sure, take the lawn mower

While most people think hard before lending their own possessions, they are often more amenable to lending things that don't belong to them. This must have been true during Roman times if we can judge from this proverb, literally "it's easy to be generous with another person's property."

facinus quos inquinat aequat
FAH-kih-nuus kwohs IN-kwih-naht Ī-kwaht
a criminal is a criminal is a criminal

A maxim of Lucan, "crime levels those whom it contaminates," telling us that anyone guilty of a crime—no matter how petty—is still to be regarded as a criminal. Thus, white collars, blue collars, and blazer collars all stain.

facta sunt potentiora verbis
FAH-ktah suunt poh-ten-tee-OH-rah WEHR-bees
don't talk of love, show me!

This proverb, literally "deeds are more powerful than words," teaches that what we actually do makes a much greater impression than what we say. Modern government leaders who talk a good game but never get around to accomplishing what they promise will quickly lose popular support as they confirm the validity of *facta sunt potentiora verbis*.

fac ut sciam
fahk uut SKEE-ahm
don't leave me in the dark

Also translated as "tell me," and more literally as "make me be aware."

faex populi
fĭks PAW-puu-lee
the rabble

Cicero's phrase for "the common people," literally "the dregs of the people." The bitterness intrinsic in the phrase becomes apparent when we relate *faex* and its plural *faeces* (FĬ-kehs) to the English derivative "feces," which in Great Britain is spelled "faeces" and, like "feces," is pronounced FEE-seez. Enough said. (See also IGNOBILE VULGUS.)

fallacia alia aliam trudit
fahl-LAH-kee-ah AH-lee-ah AH-lee-ahm TROO-dit
tell one lie, then another, and another. . .

A proverb of Terence, literally "one deceit presses hard upon another." Sir Walter Scott (1771–1832) said it more memorably:

> Oh, what a tangled web we weave,
> When first we practice to deceive!

(See also SCELERE VELANDUM EST SCELUS.)

fallaci nimium ne crede lucernae
fahl-LAH-kee NIH-mih-uum nay KRAY-day luu-KEHR-nī
don't say you love her until you see her in daylight

Ovid, well aware of how flattering artificial light can be, gives practical advice to young men and old, literally "trust not too much to deceitful lamplight."

falsus in uno, falsus in omnibus
FAHL-suus in OO-noh FAHL-suus in AWM-nih-buus
your first slip robs you of your credibility

As every trial lawyer knows, an effective way to discredit testimony that may damage a case is to demonstrate to the jury that the witness has not been consistently truthful. Thus, *falsus in uno, falsus in omnibus*, "false in one thing, false in everything."

fama clamosa
FAH-mah klah-MOH-sah
the latest scandal

Literally "a noisy rumor."

fama nihil est celerius
FAH-mah NIH-hil est keh-LEH-rih-uus
nothing is swifter than rumor

See also VIRES ACQUIRIT EUNDO.

fari quae sentiat
FAH-ree kwī SEN-tih-aht
to say what one thinks

The mark of a bold person—not always esteemed by others.

fatigatis humus cubile est
fah-tee-GAH-tihs HUU-muus kuu-BEE-leh est
dead tired, you'll sleep anywhere

Literally "to the wearied the ground is a bed."

felicitas nutrix est iracundiae
fay-LEE-kih-tahs NOO-triks est ee-rah-KUUN-dih-ī
nothing like a bit of good luck to pick up the spirits

This observation, literally "prosperity is the nurse of irascibility," tells us that even an inveterate grouch will brighten up when things go his way.

ferae naturae
FEH-rī nah-TOO-rī
of an untamed nature

A legal term for an undomesticated animal or bird.

feriis caret necessitas
FAY-rih-ees KAH-ret neh-KES-sih-tahs
necessity has no holidays

feriunt summos fulgura montes
FEH-ree-uunt SUUM-maws FUUL-guu-rah MAWN-tehs
keep your powder dry and your head down

Our chances of attracting adverse criticism increase markedly when we achieve some prominence, according to this observation from Horace, literally "bolts of lightning strike the mountaintops." Most critics don't bother to attack the rest of us.

fervet opus
FEHR-wet AW-puus
I'm making progress

Virgil, reporting that a project is moving briskly forward, literally "the work glows."

fessus viator
FES-suus wee-AH-tawr
a weary traveler

festinatio tarda est
fes-tee-NAH-tih-oh TAHR-dah est
more haste, less speed

Advice often given and often ignored, literally "haste is late."

fiat experimentum in corpore vili
FEE-aht eks-peh-ree-MEN-tuum in KAWR-paw-reh WEE-lih
don't experiment on things of value

Good advice, literally "let an experiment be made on a worthless body (or object)."

fidelis ad urnam
fih-DAY-lihs ahd UUR-nahm
true till death

Friendship or love can't ask for greater constancy, literally "faithful to the (funerary) urn."

fidem qui perdit nihil ultra perdere potest
FIH-daym kwee PEHR-dit NIH-hil UUL-trah PEHR-deh-reh POH-test
above all, guard your credit rating

Publilius Syrus offering all entrepreneurs excellent advice, "he (or she) who loses credit can lose nothing further."

fide, sed cui vide
FIH-day sed KOO-ee WEE-deh
trust, but take care whom (you trust)

fides facit fidem
FIH-days FAH-kit FIH-dem
trust begets trust

Trust is a two-way street, according to this proverb, literally "faith creates faith."

fidus et audax
FEE-duus et OW-dahks
faithful and bold

filius nullius
FEE-lee-uus nuul-LEE-uus
a bastard

This term, literally "a son of nobody," is also given as **filius populi** (PAW-puu-lee), with the meaning "bastard" and translated literally as "a son of the people."

finis ecce laborum!
FEE-nihs EK-keh lah-BOH-ruum
behold the end of our labors!

See also ERGO BIBAMUS.

flamma fumo est proxima
FLAHM-mah FOO-moh est PRAW-ksih-mah
where there's smoke, there's fire

Plautus, telling us literally "flame is very close to fire," so if you smell smoke you had better believe that something is on fire. Likewise, if you suspect that skulduggery is afoot, you had better investigate.

flecti, non frangi
FLEK-tee nohn FRAHN-gee
to bend, not to break

The motto of someone who is willing to accommodate change, but not willing to give up.

flos iuventutis (or juventutis)
flohs yuu-wehn-TOO-tihs
the flower of youth

forma bonum fragile est
FAWR-mah BAW-nuum FRAH-gih-leh est
beauty is a fleeting blessing

Ovid, on the transitory nature of good looks. (See also FORMA FLOS, FAMA FLATUS.)

forma flos, fama flatus
FAWR-mah flohs FAH-mah FLAH-tuus
beauty is a flower, fame a breath

And this compounds the despair inherent in FORMA BONUM FRAGILE EST.

forte scutum, salus ducum
FAWR-teh SKOO-tuum SAH-luus DUU-kuum
a strong shield is the safety of leaders

Another argument for the efficacy of building armies rather than providing for the needs of ordinary people. This argument may be more true for despots than for leaders of enlightened democracies.

fortuna favet fatuis
fawr-TOO-nah FAH-wet FAH-too-ees
fortune favors fools

fortuna multis dat nimium, nulli satis
fawr-TOO-nah MUUL-tihs daht NIH-mih-uum NUUL-lih SAH-tihs
no one ever is given too much

When gamblers win a trifecta, they fret at not having bet twice as much as they did. Martial makes this attitude clear in this adage, literally "to many fortune gives too much, to none enough."

fraus pia
frows PEE-ah
a pious fraud

> The worst kind. Also given as PIA FRAUS.

fructu non foliis arborem aestima
FROO-ktuu nohn FAW-lih-ees AHR-bawr-em Ī-stih-mah
judge by results, not by appearances

> Phaedrus cautioning us to "judge a tree by its fruit, not by its leaves."

frustra laborat qui omnibus placere studet
FROO-strah lah-BOH-raht kwee AWM-nih-buus PLAH-keh-reh STUU-det
you can't please the entire world

> A proverb worthy of keeping in mind, literally "he labors in vain who strives to please everybody."

fugere est triumphus
FUU-geh-reh est tree-UUM-fuus
to flee is a triumph

> Under the appropriate circumstances. Consider the words of Shakespeare's Falstaff: "The better part of valor is discretion; in the which better part I have saved my life." And if you need a jingle to recite while you are fleeing, recall:

> > He that fights and runs away
> > Lives to fight another day.

furari litoris arenas
foo-RAH-rih LEE-tawr-ihs ah-RAY-nahs

to undertake a never-ending task

> Literally "to steal the sands of the seashore."

G

Gallia est omnis divisa in partes tres
GAHL-lee-ah est AWM-nees dee-WEE-sah in PAHR-tays trays

all Gaul is divided into three parts

> The opening sentence of Julius Caesar's *Commentaries on the Gallic War*—the start of every budding Latinist's long journey through the literature of ancient Rome.

gaudet tentamine virtus
GOW-deht ten-TAH-mih-neh WIHR-toos

always ready to be tested

> Literally "manhood rejoices in trial." *Tentamine* is also given as **temptamine** (tem-PTAH-mih-neh), also meaning "in trial."

gaudium certaminis
GOW-dih-uum kehr-TAH-mih-nihs

the joy of battle

> This phrase, also given as CERTAMINIS GAUDIA, gives us one insight into the differences between the ancient Romans and today's Americans. While we are said to be preoccupied with the joys of sex, the Romans spoke of the joy of battle.

gens bracata
gayns brah-KAH-tah

civilians

In Roman times, when clothes really made the man, Gauls and barbarians dressed differently from Roman citizens. So the common folk were *gens bracata*, literally "trousered persons," while Roman citizens were **gens togata** (taw-GAH-tah), literally "togaed persons."

genus est mortis male vivere
GEH-nuus est MAWR-tihs MAH-leh WEE-weh-reh
behave yourself

> Good counsel from Ovid, "to live evilly is a kind of death."

gloria virtutis umbra
GLOH-ree-ah wihr-TOO-tihs UUM-brah
glory is the shadow of virtue

> The Romans made much of virtue. (See, for example, the many entries beginning with VIRTUS.)

gradatim
grah-DAH-tim
gradually *or* step by step

> Thus the assertion **gradatim vincimus** (WIHN-kih-muus), freely translated as "we conquer by degrees." As long as we are patient, we need not overwhelm an enemy.

gradu diverso, via una
GRAH-doo dee-WEHR-soh WEE-ah OO-nah
pursuing the same goal, but with a different timetable

> This phrase, literally "with different pace, (but) on one road," comes in handy when, for example, two or more scientists, social reformers, or the like are working independently toward identical goals.

Graecia capta ferum victorem cepit

GRĪ-kee-ah KAH-ptah FEH-ruum wih-KTOH-rem KAY-peet

captive Greece took captive its uncivilized victor

This from Horace, who understood what really matters once armed combat ends. While the Romans many times, but not always, defeated the Greeks in battle, the Romans eventually saw that much of the Greek culture had made an indelible mark on Rome. So, in the end, the defeated Greeks were the real winners.

gratia gratiam parit

GRAH-tee-ah GRAH-tee-ahm PAH-riht

kindness begets kindness

Always? Let's hope so.

gratis dictum

GRAH-tees DIH-ktuum

a mere assertion

Literally "a gratuitous statement," unsupported by evidence and so not to be taken as necessarily valid. For example, consider "We will certainly honor the truce we offer."

gratis pro Deo

GRAH-tees proh DAY-oh

free of cost

Literally "for God's sake."

grave delictum

GRAH-weh day-LIH-ktuum

a grave offense

graviora manent
grah-wee-OH-rah MAH-nent
the worst is yet to come

A dire prediction from Virgil, "more grievous perils remain."

graviora quaedam sunt remedia periculis
grah-wee-OH-rah KWĪ-dahm suunt reh-MEH-dee-ah peh-REE-kuu-lees
maybe you ought to get a second opinion

Publilius Syrus telling us "some remedies are worse than the dangers"—of a disease, that is. But we can surely apply this observation to many proffered solutions to many perceived problems.

gravis ira regum est semper
GRAH-wihs EE-rah RAY-guum est SEM-pehr
the wrath of kings is always heavy

Seneca telling us not to fool around with kings or other powerful persons or institutions.

gregatim
greh-GAH-tihm
in crowds

But also translated as "in herds" and "in droves" and "in flocks."

gutta cavat lapidem, consumitur anulus usu
GUUT-tah KAH-waht LAH-pih-dem kohn-SOO-mih-tuur AH-nuu-luus OO-soo
patience and persistence

This proverb, literally "a drop hollows out stone, a ring is worn away by use," tells us that great things can be accomplished through continuing small efforts applied assiduously over time. (See also PARVIS E GLANDIBUS QUERCUS.)

H

habet et musca splenum
HAH-bet et MUU-skah SPLAY-nuum
even the least of us can be irritable

Literally "even a fly has its spleen." So be cautious in dealing with the weak.

hac urget lupus, hac canis
hahk UUR-get LOO-puus hahk KAH-nihs
in deep trouble

Horace giving politicians and the rest of us a metaphor for any situation that appears to be hopeless, literally "on this side a wolf presses, on that a dog."

haec nugae in seria ducent mala
hīk NOO-gī in SAY-ree-ah DOO-kent MAH-lah
stay clear of that slippery slope

Horace, in "these trifles will lead to serious evils," offering good counsel against committing even the slightest of moral, ethical, or professional missteps. (See also OMNE VITIUM IN PROCLIVI EST and PRINCIPIIS OBSTA.)

haec tibi dona fero
hīk TIH-bih DOH-nah FEH-roh
these gifts I bear to thee

Motto of Newfoundland.

haud passibus aequis
howd PAHS-sih-buus Ī-kwees
with unequal steps

More literally "not with equal steps" or "with steps by no means equal." A phrase adapted from Virgil's **non passibus aequis**, with the meaning "not with equal steps." In both forms, the intent is to suggest slower progress, in that steps taken turn out to be shorter than steps previously taken.

helluo librorum
HEHL-loo-oh lih-BRAWR-uum
a bookworm

More literally "a devourer of books" or "a glutton for books."

heredem Deus facit, non homo
HAY-ray-dem DAY-uus FAH-kit nohn HAW-moh
God makes the heir, not man

You never know how your children will turn out, no matter how patient you are with them.

heu, vitam perdidi, operose nihil agendo
hehoo WEE-tahm PEHR-dih-dee aw-peh-ROH-seh NIH-hil ah-GEN-doh
I could have been a contender

A complaint occasionally and literally expressed as "alas, I have wasted my life, busily doing nothing."

hiatus valde deflendus
hee-AH-tuus WAHL-day day-FLAYN-duus
long time no see

What do you say or write when you have put off for too long a call or a letter to an old friend? Here's a good phrase designed to get you off the hook, literally "a gap greatly to be lamented." Not to worry. Good friends will always forgive you.

hic funis nihil attraxit
heek FOO-nihs NIH-hil aht-TRAH-ksit
the scheme is a failure

Literally "this line has taken no fish." Apparently, ancient Romans were no different than Americans in thinking that suckers can fall for a line.

hic iacet (or jacet) lepus
heek YAH-ket LEH-puus
here's the problem

Literally "here lies the hare."

hinc lucem et pocula sacra
hihnk LOO-kem et POH-kuu-lah SAH-krah
from here (we receive) light and sacred libations

Motto of Cambridge University. For this I sent my children to college?

his non obstantibus
hees nohn awb-STAHN-tih-buus
notwithstanding these obstructions

historia vero testis temporum, lux veritatis
hih-STAW-ree-ah WAY-roh TES-tihs TEM-paw-ruum luuks way-rih-TAH-tihs
posterity will figure it all out

Valuable insight from Cicero, literally "history is indeed the witness of the times, the light of truth." But what about all those revisionists who rewrite or reinterpret history? They would say they've figured it all out. Historians continue to disagree.

hoc habet
hohk HAH-bet
he's had it

When Roman spectators at a gladiatorial contest—actually a fight to the death—yelled *hoc habet*, literally "he has it," they meant "he is hit," and a hit in such encounters meant the poor fellow would not live to fight again.

hoc sensu
hohk SAYN-soo
in this sense

hoc sustinete maius ne veniat malum
hohk suus-tih-NAY-teh MAH-yuus nay WAY-nee-aht MAH-luum
cop a plea

Advice from Phaedrus on the terrible things that befall humans, literally "endure this evil lest a greater (evil) come upon you."

hoc tempore
hohk TEM-paw-reh
at this time

hominibus plenum, amicis vacuum
haw-MIH-nih-buus PLAY-nuum ah-MEE-kees WAH-koo-uum
a true friend is hard to find

Apparently even for Seneca, who said his world was literally "full of people, empty of friends."

homini ne fides nisi cum quo modium salis absumpseris

HAW-mih-nee nay FIH-days NIH-sih kuum kwoh MAW-dee-uum SAH-lihs ahb-SOOM-pseh-rees

take your time in judging people

Literally "trust no man unless you have consumed a peck of salt with him," a maxim that is down-to-earth, downright up-to-date, and down on first impressions. When you consider that a peck is a quarter of a bushel, it would take dozens and dozens of highly seasoned power lunches to consume a peck of salt with anyone. By then, surely, you would be able to trust your judgment. (See also DECIPIT FRONS PRIMA MULTA.)

hominis est errare, insipientis perseverare

HAW-mih-nihs est ehr-RAH-reh een-sih-pee-EN-tihs pehr-seh-way-RAH-reh

once is enough

This Roman proverb, "it is for man to err, for a fool to persist," adjures us not to make the same mistake twice.

homo homini aut deus aut lupus

HAW-moh HAW-mih-nee owt DAY-uus owt LOO-puus

man is to man either a god or a wolf

Is there nothing in between?

homo multarum litterarum

HAW-moh muul-TAH-ruum lit-teh-RAH-ruum

a learned person

Also rendered as "a man of much learning" and literally as "a man of many letters." This phrase is not the source of the English phrase "man of letters," denoting an author or literary scholar.

homo nullius coloris
HAW-moh NUUL-lee-uus kaw-LOH-rihs

an uncertain quantity

This phrase, literally "a man of no color," can be used to indicate "a man of no political party" or more generally "a man whose opinions are unknown" or "an unknown person."

homo sui iuris (or juris)
HAW-moh SOO-ee YOO-rihs

an independent man

Literally "a man of his own law," in the sense that he is his own master, not subservient to others.

homo trium litterarum
HAW-moh TREE-uum lit-teh-RAH-ruum

a thief

This phrase—a jocular allusion to HOMO MULTARUM LITTER-ARUM, "a man of many letters"—translates literally as "a man of three letters." And all Romans knew that the three letters were **f u r**, and **fur** (foor) in Latin means "thief."

honesta mors turpi vita potior
haw-NEH-stah mawrs TUUR-pee WEE-tah PAW-tih-awr

an honorable death is better than a disgraceful life

Tacitus, perhaps speaking for many of us.

honores mutant mores
haw-NOH-rehs MOO-tahnt MOH-rehs

honors alter character

Unfortunately, some people who rise to the top may forget how hard they struggled to achieve success and then do nothing to help those who are still struggling.

honos habet onus

HAW-nohs HAH-bet AW-nuus

honor carries responsibility

> Literally "honor has its burden."

horae subsicivae

HOH-rī suub-sih-KEE-wī

free hours

> Leisure time.

hos ego versiculos feci, tulit alter honores

hohs EH-goh wehr-SIH-kuu-lohs FAY-kee TOO-leet AHL-tehr haw-NOH-rehs

I wrote these insignificant lines of verse, another person took the credit

> Virgil crying plagiarism.

hospes, hostis

HAW-spehs HAW-stihs

a stranger, an enemy

> Expressing an attitude still prevalent in many cultures.

hostis honori invidia

HAW-stihs haw-NOH-rih in-WIH-dee-ah

envy is the foe of esteem

humani nihil alienum

hoo-MAH-nih NIH-hil ah-lee-AY-nuum

nothing human is foreign to me

> A maxim adapted from Terence.

I

ibit eo quo vis qui zonam perdidit
EE-bit AY-oh kwoh wees kwee ZOH-nahm PEHR-dih-dit
he who pays the piper may call the tune

Horace, who knew his way around, telling us literally that "he who has lost his money belt will go wherever you wish."

idem velle et idem nolle
EE-dem WEL-leh et EE-dem NOHL-leh
to like and dislike the same things

Kindred spirits in a happy relationship.

id facere laus est quod decet, non quod licet
id FAH-keh-reh lows est kwawd DEH-ket nohn kwawd LIH-ket
not merely legal, but also ethical

A proverb from Seneca, literally "he merits praise who does what he ought to do, not what he is allowed to do."

idoneus homo
ih-DOH-nay-uus HAW-moh
a man of proven ability

Literally "a fit man."

ieiunus (or jejunus) raro stomachus vulgaria temnit
yay-OON-uus RAH-roh STAW-mah-kuus wuul-GAH-ree-ah TEM-nit
beggars can't be choosers

Horace, realistic as usual, telling us literally that "an empty stomach seldom scorns ordinary food."

ignavis semper feriae sunt
ih-GNAH-wihs SEM-pehr FAY-rih-ī suunt
to the lazy, it's always holiday time

ignobile vulgus
ih-GNOH-bih-leh WUUL-guus
the rabble

Literally "the ignoble populace." Also translated as "the baseborn multitude." (For an even more contemptuous term, see FAEX POPULI.)

ignoscito saepe alteri numquam tibi
ih-GNOHS-kih-toh SĪ-peh AHL-teh-ree NUUM-kwahm TIH-bih
forgive others often, yourself never

ille crucem sceleris pretium tulit, hic diadema
IL-leh KRUU-kem SKEH-lehr-ihs PREH-tee-uum TOO-leet heek dee-ah-DAY-mah
the law does not treat all people fairly

Juvenal observing sardonically, "that man got the cross (crucifixion) as the reward for crime, this man a crown."

ille dolet vere qui sine teste dolet
IL-leh DAW-let WAY-ray kwee SIH-neh TES-teh DAW-let
true grief is private

We are told by Martial to distrust public displays of grief, literally "that person truly grieves who grieves alone." Tell it to the staffs of TV news programs. Surely TV viewers can grasp death or misfortune without being exposed to intrusive close-ups of the faces of anguished families of the victims.

illotis manibus
il-LOH-tihs MAHN-ih-buus
unprepared

> Literally "with unwashed hands."

imagines maiorum
ih-MAH-gih-nehs mī-OH-ruum
portraits of ancestors

imitatores, servum pecus
ih-mih-tah-TOH-rehs SEHR-wuum PEH-kuus
don't be a copycat

Imitation has been called the sincerest form of flattery, but not by Horace, here venting his spleen on lesser writers who preyed on him, addressing them literally as "you imitators, a slavish herd." (See also O IMITATORES, SERVUM PECUS.)

impavidum ferient ruinae
im-PAH-wih-duum FEH-rih-ent roo-IN-ī
nothing can shatter the steadfastness of an upright man

Horace indulging in hyperbole on the character of a righteous person, literally "the ruins (of the world) will strike him undaunted."

imperat aut servit collecta pecunia cuique
IM-peh-raht owt SEHR-wit kawl-LAY-ktah peh-KOO-nee-ah KOO-ee-kweh
money amassed either rules or serves us

Horace warning us to maintain control over our wealth lest it control us.

implicite
im-PLIH-kih-tay
by implication

impos animi
IM-paws AH-nih-mee
feeble-minded

Literally "not master over (one's) mind."

impotens sui
IM-paw-tayns SOO-ee
lacking self-control

imprimatur
im-prih-MAH-tuur
let it be printed

This is the term used by ecclesiastical authorities in granting permission for publication of a book, pamphlet, etc. It has been taken into English with the same pronunciation and the meaning of "official sanction by any authorized body," as in "The National Cancer Institutes refused to give the research paper its imprimatur."

imprimis
im-PREE-mees
in the first place

Also taken as "especially" and "first in order."

in aere piscari, in mare venari
in AH-ay-reh pihs-KAH-ree in MAH-reh way-NAH-ree
to chase rainbows

This metaphor, literally "to fish in the air, to hunt in the sea," applies to any pursuit of an impossible dream.

in aqua scribis
in AH-kwah SKREE-bihs
you are writing in water

A way of telling a person that he or she is wasting time on something that will not endure.

in arena aedificas
in ah-RAY-nah ī-DIH-fih-kahs
building castles in the air

This phrase, literally "you're building on sand," is useful in dismissing an idea or plan that is perceived as being impracticable. (See also IN AREA PISCARI, IN MARE VENARI.)

in caducum parietem inclinare
in kah-DOO-kuum pah-rih-EH-tem in-klih-NAH-reh
to lean against a falling wall

A metaphor for an action based on misplaced faith.

incredulus odi
in-KRAY-duu-luus OH-dee
being skeptical, I detest it

An example from Horace of the compactness of Latin, which makes it possible to say much in few words.

incudi reddere
in-KOO-dee REHD-deh-reh
to touch up *or* to revise

Horace, who understood that it takes more than one draft to knock out polished verse, gave us this metaphor, literally "to return to the anvil."

incurvat genus senectus
in-KUUR-waht GEH-nuus seh-NEK-toos
old age bends the knee

With advancing years most of us become more submissive to the wishes of others than we were when we were in our primes. Maybe.

in Deo speramus
in DAY-oh spay-RAH-muus
in God we hope

> Motto of Brown University.

indictum sit
in-DIH-ktuum sit
bite your tongue

> Literally "let it be unsaid."

in diem vivere
in DEE-em WEE-weh-reh
to live from hand to mouth

Literally "to live for today," telling us that when we scarcely have enough to get by on even for one day, there's no point in discussing retirement plans.

inedita
in-AY-dih-tah
unpublished works

> A bibliographic term.

inest sua gratia parvis
EEN-est SOO-ah GRAH-tih-ah PAHR-wihs
even little things have a charm of their own

in fine
in FEE-neh
in the end

The origin of the English expression "in fine" (fīn), meaning "briefly" or "in short."

ingens telum necessitas
IN-gayns TAY-luum neh-KES-sih-tahs
necessity is the mother of invention

Literally "necessity is a powerful weapon." (For a second phrase meaning "necessity is the mother of invention," see NECESSITAS RATIONEM INVENTRIX.)

iniquum petas ut aequum feras
in-EE-kwuum PEH-tahs uut Ī-kwuum FEH-rahs
the gentle art of haggling

Insurance lawyers and literary agents surely have learned this Latin phrase, literally "ask for what is unreasonable so that you may obtain what is just."

in nihilum nil posse reverti
in NIH-hih-luum neel PAWS-seh reh-WEHR-tee
matter is indestructible

The perception by Persius that literally "there is nothing that can be reduced to nothing."

in nocte consilium
in NAW-kteh kohn-SIH-lee-uum
the night brings counsel

Or, as we would say idiomatically, "it's best to sleep on the matter."

in nuce
in NUU-keh
in a nutshell

in oculis civium
in AW-kuu-lees KEE-wih-uum
in public

> Literally "in the eyes of citizens."

inops, potentem dum vult imitari, perit
IN-awps paw-TEN-tem duum wuult ih-mih-TAH-ree
PEHR-eet
don't spend beyond your means

> Phaedrus telling us literally "a poor man perishes when he tries to imitate a powerful man."

in pace leones, in proelio cervi
in PAH-keh lay-OH-nehs in PROY-lee-oh KEHR-wee
it's easy to talk a good game

> Blustering patriots who continually speak of going to war but run when conflict is imminent may be characterized as here, literally "lions in peace, deer in battle."

in poculis
in POH-kuu-lees
while drinking

> Literally "in (one's) cups." Of course, when we say in English that a person is "in his cups," we are indicating that he is drunk, and *in poculis* may be interpreted in the same way.

in proverbium cessit, sapientiam vino adumbrari
in proh-WEHR-bee-uum KES-sit sah-pee-EN-tee-ahm
WEE-noh ah-duum-BRAH-ree
don't take up serious matters when you drink

> This is Pliny the Elder telling us literally "it has become a proverb that wisdom is obscured by wine."

in silvam ligna ferre
in SIL-wahm LIH-gnah FEHR-reh
to carry coals to Newcastle

> Literally "to carry wood to the forest." (See also PISCEM NATARE DOCES.)

integra mens augustissima possessio
IN-teh-grah mehns ow-guus-TEES-sih-mah paws-SEHS-see-oh
a sound mind is the most majestic possession

in tenebris
in TEH-neh-brihs
in a state of doubt

> Literally "in darkness."

inter canem et lupum
IN-tehr KAH-nem et LOO-puum
twilight

> This phrase, literally "between a dog and a wolf," also means "between two difficulties" as well as "twilight." (See also HAC URGET LUPUS, HAC CANIS.)

interdum stultus opportuna loquitur
in-TEHR-duum STUUL-tuus awp-pawr-TOO-nah LAW-kwih-tuur
sometimes (even) a fool says something useful

intra parietes
IN-trah pah-rih-EH-tehs
within the walls (of a house or other building)

> The principal reason for including this phrase is to call attention to the Latin noun *paries*, meaning "wall," and so

shed light on the English phrase "parietal rules"—we also think of them as "house rules"—that bedevils undergraduates on so many American campuses, who mistakenly think "parietal" pertains to parenting.

intra verba peccare
IN-trah WEHR-bah pek-KAH-reh
to offend in words only

Not in actions, that is.

invictus maneo
in-WEE-ktuus MAH-nay-oh
I remain unconquered *or* I remain unbeaten

invidia gloriae comes
in-WIH-dee-ah GLOH-ree-ī KAW-mehs
envy is glory's companion

Too often true.

in vota miseros ultimus cogit timor
in WOH-tah MEE-seh-raws UUL-tih-muus KOH-git TIH-mawr
there are no atheists in foxholes

Nor were there in ancient Rome, according to Seneca, who told us "fear of death drives the wretched to make vows to the gods."

irritabis crabrones
ih-rih-TAH-bihs krah-BROH-nehs
you will stir up the hornets

A warning from Plautus to beware of those who have the capacity to sting. Could he have been thinking of censors, political rivals, or literary critics?

iudex (or judex) damnatur cum nocens absolvitur
YOO-deks DAHM-nah-tuur kuum NAW-kayns ahb-
SAWL-wih-tuur
the judge is condemned when a criminal is set free

Publilius Syrus giving us his notion of where the blame lies
when we disagree with a verdict. Today we can blame laws
that appear to favor the rights of criminals over those of victims.

iugulare (or jugulare) mortuos
yuu-guu-LAH-reh MAWR-too-ohs
carrying bloodshed to new heights

We read of acts of murder that appear to grow more
extreme each day, so repulsive that we lack words to describe
them. In *iugulare mortuos*, literally "to cut the throats of the
dead," the Romans gave us chilling words that may suffice for
a while at least.

iure (or jure) divino
YOO-reh dih-WEE-noh
by divine right *or* by divine law

ius (or jus) gentium
yoos GEN-tee-uum
international law

Literally "the law of nations."

ius (or jus) naturale
yoos nah-too-RAH-leh
natural law

ius (or jus) scriptum
yoos SKRIH-ptuum
written law

J

jejunus raro stomachus vulgaria temnit

See IEIUNUS RARO STOMACHUS VULGARIA TEMNIT.

judex damnatur cum nocens absolvitur

See IUDEX DAMNATUR CUM NOCENS ABSOLVITUR.

jugulare mortuos

See IUGULARE MORTUOS.

jure divino

See IURE DIVINO.

jus gentium

See IUS GENTIUM.

jus naturale

See IUS NATURALE.

jus scriptum

See IUS SCRIPTUM.

L

labor ipse voluptas
LAH-bawr IH-pseh waw-LUU-ptahs
labor itself is pleasure

For people who love their work, at least.

laborum dulce lenimen
lah-BOH-ruum DUUL-keh lay-NEE-men
sweet solace of my toils

Horace, addressing his lyre, gives us a saccharine phrase to use when turning to a pet dog, a piece of tatting, a violin, or the like while taking a break from a demanding intellectual or creative project.

lacrimis oculos suffusa nitentis
LAH-krih-mihs AW-kuu-lohs suuf-FOO-sah nih-TEN-tihs
her sparkling eyes bedewed with tears

A lovely image from Virgil.

lapis philosophorum
LAH-pihs fih-law-saw-FAWR-uum
the philosopher's stone

This is the hypothetical substance sought by ancient alchemists in the expectation that it would enable them to convert base metals into gold.

Latine dictum
lah-TEE-neh DIH-ktuum
spoken in Latin

lato sensu
LAH-toh SAYN-soo
in a broad sense

The opposite of STRICTO SENSU.

latrante uno, latrat statim et alter canis
lah-TRAHN-teh OO-noh LAH-traht STAH-tim et AHL-tehr KAH-nihs
everybody wants to get into the act

The thought expressed literally here is that "when one dog barks, another dog immediately barks." But the point of the adage is that when an influential columnist or critic, for example, attacks a new idea, op-ed pages suddenly bloom with verbiage from writers of lesser standing' who suddenly discover that they too disapprove of the idea.

laudari a viro laudato
low-DAH-ree ah WEE-roh low-DAH-toh
to be praised by someone who is himself praised

Far better than being praised by someone who has no standing.

laudumque immensa cupido
low-DUUM-kweh ihm-MAYN-sah kuu-PEE-doh
and a boundless desire for praise

Virgil being critical of those who have a passion for renown.

laus propria sordet
lows PROH-pree-ah SAWR-det
self-praise is debasing

legant prius et postea despiciant
LEH-gahnt PREE-uus et PAW-stay-ah day-SPIH-kih-ahnt
but you haven't even read the book

The writer's lament upon receiving poor reviews, literally "let them read first and despise afterward."

legenda
leh-GEN-dah
things to be read

leges mori serviunt
LAY-gehs MOH-ree SEHR-wee-uunt
laws are subservient to custom

Suggesting that good laws are based on actual practices, not on grand philosophic ideas.

leone fortior fides
lay-OH-neh FAWR-tee-awr FIH-days
faith is stronger than a lion

After a manner of speaking.

leve fit quod bene fertur onus
LEH-weh feet kwawd BEH-neh FEHR-tuur AW-nuus
enjoy your work

Ovid telling us that "a load cheerfully borne becomes light."

lex uno ore omnes alloquitur
layks OO-noh OH-reh AWM-nehs ahl-LOH-kwee-tuur
everyone is equal before the law

Literally "the law speaks with one mouth to all." At least we hope it does.

liberavi animam meam
lee-behr-AH-wee AN-nih-mahm MAY-ahm
now it's off my mind

Literally "I have freed my mind" or "I am relieved." Useful for anyone who confesses guilt or complicity in an illicit plot, extramarital affair, or the like. See also ABSOLVI MEAM ANIMAM.

libertas est potestas faciendi id quod iure (or jure) licet
lee-BEHR-tahs est paw-TEHS-tahs fah-kee-EN-dee id kwawd YOO-reh LIH-ket

liberty is the power of doing what is permitted by law

limae labor et mora
LEE-mī LAH-bawr et MAWR-ah

no wonder writers never meet their deadlines

Horace writing literally of "the toil and delay of revision," by which a literary work is brought to its final, polished state. The noun *lima* (LEE-mah) translates as "revision" when used figuratively, as the tool called a "file" when used literally, so with a bit of imagination we envision serious writers applying files to their sentences in order to give them cutting edges.

limbus fatuorum
LIM-buus fah-too-AWR-uum

fools' paradise

lis litem generat
lees LEE-tem GEH-neh-raht

You started it! No, you did!

Anyone who knows anything at all about the vicissitudes of domestic life knows literally that "strife begets strife." So what is one to do? Just remember that *lis* and *litem* can also be translated as "lawsuit"—the first in the nominative case, the second in the accusative—and both suggesting imminent deep and continuing trouble. Better nip disagreements in the bud. (For an example of how little disputes can grow, see MAXIMA BELLA EX LEVISSIMA CAUSIS.)

lis litem resolvere
lees LEE-tem reh-SAWL-weh-reh

to explain one obscurity by another

This phrase literally translates as "to settle strife by strife," more broadly as "to resolve one dispute by introducing another." The end result of any of the three interpretations given here is that the parties to the dispute are no closer to a true resolution than when the process began. Now who would indulge in such folly? Nobody except for thousands of academics, literary critics, economists, government officials, theologians, Internal Revenue code writers, and a few others.

litterae scriptae manet
LIT-teh-rī SKREE-ptī MAH-net
don't put it in writing

A warning, literally "the written words endure." And if the Romans had been more advanced in technology, they would also have cautioned against making tape recordings of conversations.

litterae sine moribus vanae
LIT-teh-rī SIH-neh MOH-rih-buus WAH-nī
scholarship without morals is useless

Motto of the University of Pennsylvania.

longe absit!
LAWN-gay AHB-sit
God forbid!

Literally "far be it from me!"

longo sed proximus intervallo
LAWN-goh sed PRAW-ksih-muus in-tehr-WAHL-law
a poor second

Virgil's phrase, literally "the next but separated by a great distance," for anyone or anything that doesn't even come close in a competition. Recall any horse losing a race to Secretariat.

luce lucet aliena
LOO-keh LOO-ket ah-lih-AY-nah
any way you slice it, it's still plagiarism

Literally "it shines with another's light."

lucri bonus est odor
LUUK-ree BAW-nuus est AW-dawr
sweet is the odor of wealth

A maxim from Juvenal. Notwithstanding the approval of Juvenal, we too often speak of "filthy lucre," a cliché employing an English word deriving from **lucrum**, the nominative form of *lucri*, meaning "wealth." (See also ODOR LUCRI.)

ludere cum sacris
LOO-deh-reh kuum SAH-krees
to trifle with sacred things

lumen naturale
LOO-men nah-too-RAH-leh
natural intelligence

Literally "the light of nature," but also translated as "enlightenment."

lumenque inventae purpureum
LOO-men-kweh in-WEN-tī puur-PUUR-eh-uum
the radiant bloom of youth

Literally "the purple light of youth." This is Virgil waxing eloquent about the prime of life—as it was seen back in ancient Rome.

lumen soli mutuum das
LOO-men SOH-lih MOO-too-uum dahs
you're the top

> Extravagant praise, literally "you lend light to the sun."

lupa
LUU-pah
she-wolf

> But also "prostitute," leading to **lupanar** (luu-PAH-nahr), meaning "brothel."

lux in tenebris
luuks in TEH-neh-brihs
light in the darkness

lux mundi
luuks MUUN-dee
light of the world

> Jesus Christ.

M

magister caerimoniarum
mah-GIH-stehr kī-rih-moh-nih-AH-ruum
master of ceremonies

> See also REX CONVIVII.

magna civitas, magna solitudo
MAH-gnah KEE-wih-tahs MAH-gnah soh-lih-TOO-doh
a great place to visit

> In this adage, literally "a great city is a great desert," the noun *solitudo* is rendered as "desert," but it may also be taken as "loneliness."

magnae fortunae pericula

MAH-gnī fawr-TOO-nī peh-REE-kuu-lah

the dangers of great success

Tacitus gave us this phrase, and we substantiate it. Think of what has happened to so many of our overpaid sports superstars and financial wizards.

magnae spes alteri Romae

MAH-gnī spays AHL-teh-ree ROH-mī

he's a real comer

Virgil's phrase, literally "a second hope of mighty Rome," was originally said of the son of Aeneas—considered by Romans to be the founder of their nation—but it can be said of any promising young person.

magna est vis consuetudinis

MAH-gnah est wees kohn-suu-ay-TOO-dih-nihs

great is the power of habit

To provide good and not so good results.

magna servitus est magna fortuna

MAH-gnah SEHR-wih-tuus est MAH-gnah fawr-TOO-nah

a great fortune is a great slavery

Seneca warning that wealth is not an unmixed blessing. (See what Tacitus said about this in MAGNAE FORTUNAE PERICULA.)

magnas inter opes inops

MAH-gnahs IN-tehr AW-pays IN-awps

poor amid great riches

Horace reminding us that general wealth in a society does not mean that everybody shares in it. So much for trickle-down economics.

magna vis est conscientiae
MAH-gnah wees est kohn-skee-EN-tee-ī
great is the power of conscience

magno conatu magnas nugas
MAH-gnoh koh-NAH-too MAH-gnahs NOO-gahs
molehills from mountains

Terence, aware of how much time people waste on doing things that do not matter, pungently characterized this failing as "by great effort (to obtain) great trifles."

magnum vectigal est parsimonia
MAH-gnuum wek-TEE-gahl est pahr-sih-MOH-nee-ah
save money by not wasting money

Cicero, apparently expert in the art of living on a budget, tells us literally "frugality is a great income."

magnus Alexander corpore parvus erat
MAH-gnuus ah-lek-SAHN-dehr KAWR-paw-reh PAHR-wuus EH-raht
you don't have to be 7 feet tall

Literally "great Alexander was small of body." Alexander who? Alexander the Great (356-323 B.C.), the general who succeeded so well in building his empire that he became the model for many later imperialists.

maiores (or majores) pinnas nido extendisse
mī-OH-rehs PIN-nahs NEE-doh eks-ten-DEES-seh
to try to do better than one's parents

Horace, in an avian metaphor, "to have spread wings greater than the nest," that is, to soar above the status to which one was born. Apparently, Americans did not invent the American dream.

maiori (or majori) cedo
mī-OH-ree KAY-doh
I yield to a superior

A gracious way to show deference or admit defeat. (See also CONCEDO.)

malam rem cum velis honestare, improbes
MAH-lahm rem kuum WEH-lihs haw-neh-STAH-reh IM-praw-bays
a book banned in Boston will surely succeed

Publilius Syrus warning against providing publicity for ideas you oppose, "when you wish to dignify a bad thing, condemn it." Publilius would have made a first-class public relations expert.

male imperando summum imperium amittitur
MAH-leh im-peh-RAHN-doh SUUM-uum im-PEH-rih-uum ah-MIT-tih-tuur
through misrule the greatest power can be lost

Publilius Syrus, this time offering political advice. (See also MALAM REM CUM VELIS HONESTARE, IMPROBES.)

male narrando fabula depravatur
MAH-leh nahr-RAHN-doh FAH-buu-lah day-prah-WAH-tuur
a story is spoiled by bad telling

Watch the timing and don't forget the punch line.

male parta, male dilabuntur
MAH-leh PAHR-tah MAH-leh dee-lah-BUUN-tuur
easy come, easy go

Literally "things ill gained are ill lost."

malignum spernere vulgus
mah-LIH-gnuum SPEHR-neh-reh WUUL-guus
to scorn the ill-natured crowd

mali principii malus finis
MAH-lee preen-KIH-pih-ee MAH-luus FEE-nihs
from a bad beginning a bad ending

For a related observation, see BONI PRINCIPII FINIS BONUS.

malo mori quam foedari
MAH-loh MAW-ree kwahm foy-DAH-ree
death before dishonor

Literally "I had rather die than be disgraced."

malum est consilium quod mutari non potest
MAH-luum est kohn-SIH-lee-uum kwawd moo-TAH-ree
nohn PAW-test
stay loose

Publilius Syrus offering a slogan for pragmatists, literally "it
is a bad plan that cannot be changed."

malum quia prohibitum
MAH-luum KWEE-ah praw-HIH-bih-tuum
an action wrong because it is prohibited

Not because it is immoral.

malum vas non frangitur
MAH-luum wahs nohn FRAHN-gih-tuur
a worthless dish is not broken

A slogan for butterfingers.

malus animus
MAH-luus AH-nih-muus
evil intent

malus pudor
MAH-luus PUU-dawr
false modesty

mania a potu
MAH-nee-ah ah POH-too
delirium tremens

> Literally "madness from drinking."

manu forti
MAH-noo FAWR-tee
forcible entry

> A legal term, literally "with a strong hand."

manu militari
MAH-noo mee-lih-TAH-ree
by armed force

> Literally "by the military hand."

manus e nubibus
MAH-nuus ay NOO-bih-buus
a lucky break

> Literally "a hand from the clouds."

manus manum lavat
MAH-nuus MAH-nuum LAH-waht
one hand washes the other

> You help me, I help you.

marginalia
mahr-gih-NAH-lee-ah
marginal notes

Also "peripheral things."

Mars gravior sub pace latet
mahrs GRAH-wee-awr suub PAH-keh LAH-tet
the devil is in the details

Literally "a more serious war lies hidden in the peace," in
the peace treaty, that is.

mater artium necessitas
MAH-tehr AHR-tee-uum neh-KES-sih-tahs
necessity is the mother of the arts

Another way of saying "necessity is the mother of invention." (See also INGENS TELUM NECESSITAS.)

maxima bella ex levissima causis
MAH-ksih-mah BEL-lah eks leh-WIHS-sih-mah KOW-sihs
the greatest wars arise from very slight causes

Or, as we say, "one thing leads to another." (See also LIS
LITEM GENERAT.)

maxima debetur puero reverentia
MAH-ksih-mah DAY-beh-tuur POO-eh-roh reh-weh-
REN-tee-ah
the greatest respect is due a child

Juvenal said this, and many of us have been repeating it
ever since.

maximum remedium irae mora est
MAH-ksih-muum reh-MEH-dee-uum EE-rī MAW-rah est
take time to cool off

Seneca counseling that "the greatest remedy for anger is delay." Shout it from the rooftops.

maximus in minimis
MAH-ksih-muus in MIH-nih-mees
very great in very small things

Motto of a nitpicker.

mea virtute me involvo
MAY-ah wihr-TOO-teh may in-WAWL-woh
I wrap myself up in my virtue

Horace, like so many of his contemporaries, saw virtue as redeeming. Rush Limbaugh, are you listening? (See, for example, DOMAT OMNIA VIRTUS.)

medicus curat, natura sanat
MEH-dih-kuus KOO-raht nah-TOO-rah SAH-naht
the physician treats, nature cures

medium tenuere beati
MEH-dee-uum teh-NOO-eh-reh beh-AH-tee
happy are they who have kept a middle course

Counsel for those who don't go too far to the left or right.

melioribus annis
meh-lee-OH-rih-buus AHN-nihs
in happier times

A phrase from Virgil, literally "in the better years."

memorabilia
meh-moh-rah-BEE-lee-ah
things worth remembering

Giving us the English word "memorabilia," pronounced meh-mawr-ə-BIH-lee-ə.

mens divinior
mehns dee-WEE-nih-awr
an inspired soul

A phrase from Horace, literally "a mind of diviner cast."

mens et manus
mehns et MAH-nuus
mind and hand

Motto of the Massachusetts Institute of Technology.

mens regnum bona possidet
mehns RAY-gnuum BAW-nah PAWS-sih-det
a good mind possesses a kingdom

Seneca on intelligence, first inherited and then applied to important matters.

mens sibi conscia recti
mehns SIH-bih KOHN-skee-ah REK-tee
a clear conscience

Virgil's phrase, literally and awkwardly "a mind aware within itself of rectitude."

mentiri splendide
men-TEE-ree SPLEN-dih-day
to deceive magnificently

Also translated as "to lie magnificently."

mentis gratissimus error
MEN-tihs grah-TEES-sih-muus EHR-rawr
a most delightful hallucination

A phrase from Horace.

meo periculo
MAY-oh peh-REE-kuu-loh
at my own risk

meo voto
MAY-oh WOH-toh
by my wish

meret qui laborat
MEH-ret kwee lah-BOH-raht
hard work commands respect

Literally "he is deserving who is industrious."

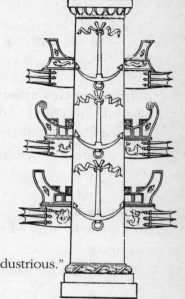

merum sal
MEH-ruum sahl
genuine wit

Literally "pure salt." (See also SAL SAPIT OMNIA.)

meum et tuum
MAY-uum et TOO-uum
mine and thine

A phrase used in law to characterize property held jointly by a couple. "The car is yours, the refrigerator is mine, and these chairs are *meum et tuum.*"

mihi cura futuri
MIH-hih KOO-rah fuu-TOO-ree
my concern is for the future

militat omnis amans
MEE-lih-taht AWM-nihs AH-mahns
love as warfare

A thought from Ovid, literally "every lover serves as a soldier." The old battle of the sexes. (See also MILITIAE SPECIES AMOR EST.)

militiae species amor est
mee-LIH-tih-ī SPEH-kih-ays AH-mawr est
love is a kind of military service

Realistic Ovid speaking again of love. (See also MILITAT OMNIS AMANS.)

mirum in modum
MEE-ruum in MAW-duum
surprisingly

Caesar's phrase, literally "in a wonderful manner."

mitis sapientia
MEE-tihs sah-pee-AYN-tee-ah
ripe wisdom *or* mellow wisdom

mole ruit sua
MOH-lay ROO-it SOO-ah
it is crushed by its own weight

A phrase from Horace, literally "it falls down of its own bulk." Useful for characterizing any overly complex argument, proposal, piece of legislation, plan, or the like.

monstrum horrendum, informe, ingens
MOHN-struum hawr-REN-duum een-FAWR-meh IN-gayns
a monster horrible, misshapen, huge

A chilling phrase from Virgil.

more maiorum (or majorum)
MOH-ray mī-OH-ruum
traditionally

> Literally "in the manner of one's ancestors."

more probato
MOH-ray praw-BAH-toh
in the approved manner

mors ianua (or janua) vitae
mawrs YAH-noo-ah WEE-tī
the end is just the beginning

> Literally "death is the gate of life." (See, for contrast, MORS ULTIMA LINEA RERUM EST.)

mors omnibus communis
mawrs OHM-nih-buus kawm-MOO-nihs
death is common to all

> Who can deny it?

mors ultima linea rerum est
mawrs UUL-tih-mah LEE-neh-ah RAY-ruum est
death is the final boundary of things

mors ultima ratio
mawrs UUL-tih-mah RAH-tee-oh
death is the final reckoning

mortuo leoni et lepores insultant
MAWR-too-oh lay-OH-nee et leh-POH-rehs een-SUUL-tahnt
even hares leap upon (*or* insult) a dead lion

This animal metaphor tells us that when a powerful leader is rendered ineffectual, even his most easily frightened opponent can muster the courage to attack him.

motu proprio
MOH-too PRAW-pree-oh
of one's own accord *or* impulse

mulier cum sola cogitat male cogitat
MUU-lee-ehr kuum SOH-lah KOH-gih-taht MAH-leh KOH-gih-taht
beware a thoughtful woman

An ill-natured observation from Publilius Syrus, literally "when a woman thinks alone she is plotting mischief."

mulier cupido quod dicit amanti in vento et rapida scribere oportet aqua
MUU-lee-ehr KUU-pih-doh kwawd DEE-kit ah-MAHN-tee in WEHN-toh et RAH-pih-dah SKREE-beh-reh aw-PAWR-teht AH-kwah
what a woman says to an ardent lover should be written on wind and running water

Catullus telling us that under demanding circumstances women do not always say precisely what they mean. Nor do men, one might hasten to add.

multa cadunt inter calicem supremaqua labra
MUUL-tah KAH-duunt IN-tehr KAH-lih-kem suu-praym-AH-kwah LAH-brah
things can go wrong at the last moment

More literally "much falls between cup and lip" or, as we commonly say, "there's many a slip 'twixt the cup and the lip."

multa docet fames
MUUL-tah DAW-ket FAH-mays

hunger teaches us many things

For a more extravagant claim, see also ETIAM STULTIS ACUIT INGENUIT FAMES.

multa petentibus desunt multa
MUUL-tah peh-TEN-tih-buus DAY-suunt MUUL-tah

to those who seek many things, many things are lacking

Horace telling us that those who covet much, are missing much.

multis utile bellum
MUUL-tihs OO-tih-leh BEL-luum

war profiteering is nothing new

Lucan telling us literally "war is profitable for many," indicating that profiteering went on even in ancient Rome.

multorum manibus magnam levatur onus
muul-TAWR-uum MAH-nih-buus MAH-gnahm leh-WAH-tuur AW-nuus

many hands make light work

Literally "by the hands of many a great load is lightened." As long as all the hands don't think they are in charge of the operation. Recall the English proverb "too many cooks spoil the broth."

multum demissus homo
MUUL-tuum day-MIHS-suus HAW-moh

a modest *or* unassuming man

A phrase from Horace.

munus Apolline dignum
MOO-nuus ah-PAWL-lih-neh DIH-gnuum
a gift worthy of Apollo

A phrase from Horace available for use in a thank-you note.

murus aeneus conscientia sana
MOO-ruus Ī-neh-uus kohn-skee-EN-tee-ah SAH-nah
a sound conscience is a wall of brass

Shakespeare said it even better when he called a quiet conscience "a peace above all earthly dignities."

muscae volitantes
MUU-skī waw-lih-TAHN-tehs
floaters

A medical term. *Muscae volitantes*, literally "flying flies," may be heard spoken in the physician's office. Commonly called "floaters," they are the moving specks many people see in their fields of vision.

mus non uni fidit antro
moos nohn OO-nee FEE-dit AHN-troh
a wise person always has a backup plan

A lesson for all of us from a little creature, literally "a mouse does not put its trust in one hole."

mutanda
moo-TAHN-dah
things to be altered

Commonly encountered in the phrase **mutatis mutandis** (moo-TAH-tees moo-TAHN-dees), literally "things having been changed that had to be changed," and freely translated as "after making the necessary changes."

mutuus consensus
MOO-too-uus kawn-SAYN-suus
mutual consent

N

nam tua res agitur paries cum proximus ardet
nahm TOO-ah rays AH-gih-tuur PAH-ree-ays kuum
PRAW-ksih-muus AHR-det
ask not for whom the bell tolls

Horace telling us literally, "when your neighbor's house is on fire, you are in danger yourself."

natale solum
nah-TAH-leh SOH-luum
native soil

One's native country.

nati natorum et qui nascentur ab illis
NAH-tee nah-TAWR-uum et kwee NAHS-kehn-tuur ahb IL-lihs
children's children and those descended from them

Virgil giving us an expressive phrase to think of when planning policies that may affect the future.

natio comoeda est
NAH-tee-oh KOH-moy-dah est
it is a nation of comic actors

Juvenal speaking of the Greeks, whom he saw as decadent.

natura abhorret a vacuo
nah-TOO-rah ahb-HAWR-ret ah WAH-koo-oh
nature abhors a vacuum

An observation advanced by Descartes.

natus ad gloriam
NAH-tuus ahd GLOH-rih-ahm
born to glory

natus nemo
NAH-tuus NAY-moh
a nobody

Literally "not a human being," a phrase from Plautus.

naufragium in portu facere
now-FRAH-gee-uum in PAWR-too FAH-keh-reh
to snatch defeat from the jaws of victory

This apt nautical metaphor, "to shipwreck in port," may be used to describe the action of anyone who manages to fail when on the verge of success. (See also NAUFRAGIUM SIBI QUISQUE FACIT.)

naufragium sibi quisque facit
now-FRAH-gee-uum SIH-bih KWIHS-kweh FAH-kit
"The fault, dear Brutus, is not in our stars,
But in ourselves. . . "

Lucan, employing a nautical metaphor, tells us we have only ourselves to blame, literally "each man makes his own shipwreck." Did Shakespeare say it better? (See also NAUFRAGIUM IN PORTU FACERE.)

nec amor nec tussis celatur
nek AH-mawr nek TUUS-sis keh-LAH-tuur
neither love nor a cough can be hidden

For the same thought expressed in plural form, see AMOR TUSSIQUE NON CELANTUR.

nec aspera terrent
nek AH-speh-rah TEHR-rent
we shall overcome

> Literally "not even hardships deter us."

nec caput nec pedes
nek KAH-puut nek PEH-days
in confusion

> Literally "neither head nor feet."

ne cede malis sed contra audientor ito
nay KAY-deh MAH-lees sed KAWN-trah ow-dee-EN-tawr EE-toh
stand tall

> Virgil counseling us to face up to adversity, literally "do not yield to misfortunes, but go more boldly to meet them."

necesse est ut multos timeat quem multi timent
neh-KES-seh est uut MUUL-tohs TIH-may-aht kwem MUUL-tee TIH-ment
he whom many fear must fear many

> Advice for tyrants from Publilius Syrus.

necessitas dat legem, non ipsa accipit
neh-KES-sih-tahs daht LAY-gehm nohn IH-psah ahk-KIH-pit
necessity recognizes no law

> Publilius Syrus telling us literally "necessity gives the law, but does not herself accept it." (For another version of the same thought, see also NECESSITAS NON HABET LEGEM.)

necessitas non habet legem
neh-KES-sih-tahs nohn HAH-bet LAY-gehm
necessity has no law

Watch out. When times are tough enough, many people will stop at nothing to keep their heads above water. (See also VENIA NECESSITATI DATUR.)

necessitas rationem inventrix
neh-KES-sih-tahs rah-tee-OH-nem in-WEN-treeks
necessity is the mother of invention

More literally "necessity is the inventor of procedures." Notice that *inventrix* is the feminine form of *inventor* (in-WEN-tawr), so the English phrase "mother of invention" is especially appropriate. (See also INGENS TELUM NECESSITAS.)

nec habeo, nec careo, nec curo
nek HAH-beh-oh nek KAH-reh-oh nek KOO-roh
I have not, I want not, I care not

Healthy adjustment to a lack of worldly goods.

nec mora nec requies
nek MAW-rah nek REH-kwih-ays
without taking a break

Virgil's phrase, literally "neither delay nor rest."

nec prece nec pretio
nek PREH-keh nek PREH-tee-oh
neither by entreaty nor by bribe

See also VEL PRECE VEL PRETIO.

nec quaerere nec spernere honorem
nek KWĪ-reh-reh nek SPEHR-neh-reh haw-NOH-rem
neither to seek nor to spurn honors

A suitable motto for any truly modest person.

ne credes laudatoribus tuis
nay KRAY-days low-dah-TAWR-ih-buus TOO-ihs
don't believe those who praise you

Don't be seduced by flattery.

nec scire fas est omnia
nek SKEE-reh fahs est AWM-nee-ah
don't be a know-it-all

Horace explaining that much knowledge is inevitably beyond human ken, literally "nor is it possible to know everything."

nec tecum possum vivere nec sine te
nek TAY-kuum PAWS-suum WEE-weh-reh nek SIH-neh tay
the forlorn cry of many who love

Martial putting into words a common plight, literally "I can neither live with you nor without you."

nec temere nec timide
nek TEH-meh-ray nek TIH-mih-day
neither rashly nor timidly

nec vixit male qui natus moriensque fefellit
nek WEE-kseet MAH-leh kwee NAH-tuus maw-ree-ENS-kweh feh-FEHL-leet
fame isn't everything

Horace telling us literally "he has not lived ill who has been born and died unnoticed."

ne facias per alium quod fieri potest per te
nay FAH-kee-ahs pehr AH-lee-uum kwawd FEE-eh-ree PAW-test pehr tay
be self-reliant

Literally "do not do through another what you can do all by yourself."

ne fronti crede
nay FRAWN-tee KRAY-day
don't judge a book by its cover

Literally "trust not in appearances." (See also BENE NATI, BENE VESTITI, ET MEDIOCRITER DOCTI.)

ne Iuppiter (or Juppiter) quidem omnibus placet
nay YOOP-pih-tehr KWEE-dem AWM-nih-buus PLAH-ket
not even Jupiter can please everyone

So do your best and don't worry.

nemo alius
NAY-moh AH-lee-uus
no one else

nemo bis punitur pro eodem delicto
NAY-moh bihs POO-nih-tuur proh eh-OH-dem day-LIK-toh
no double jeopardy

A legal principle, literally "no one is punished twice for the same offense."

nemo dat quod non habet
NAY-moh daht kwawd nohn HAH-bet
you can't get blood from a stone

   Fundraisers, pay heed to this advice, literally "no one can give what he does not have."

nemo in amore videt
NAY-moh in ah-MAWR-eh WIH-det
love is blind

   Literally "nobody in love can see."

nemo mortalium omnibus horis sapit
NAY-moh mawr-TAH-lih-uum AWM-nih-buus HOH-rihs SAH-pit
no one bats 1.000

   Pliny the Elder telling us "no mortal is always wise." The phrase *omnibus horis*, here given as "always," translates literally as "at all hours."

nemo scit praeter me ubi soccus me pressat
NAY-moh skeet PRĪ-tehr may OO-bee SAWK-kuus may PRES-saht
don't tell me what's bothering me

   Literally "no one except me knows where my shoe hurts." To keep the record straight, *soccus* translates literally as "slipper," most particularly the sock worn by actors in Roman comedies.

nemo solus satis sapit
NAY-moh SOH-luus SAH-tihs SAH-pit
two heads are better than one

   Plautus telling us literally "no one is wise enough alone."

ne nimium
nay NIH-mih-uum
do nothing to excess

> Literally "not too much."

ne prius antidotum quam venenum
nay PREE-uus ahn-tih-DOH-tuum kwahm weh-NAY-nuum
if it ain't broke, don't fix it

> Literally "not the antidote before the poison." (See also
> QUIETA NON MOVERE.)

ne puero gladium
nay POO-eh-roh GLAH-dee-uum
don't give a man's job to a boy

> Literally "(trust) not a sword to a boy."

nervi belli, pecunia infinita
NEHR-wee BEL-lee peh-KOO-nee-ah in-FEE-nih-tah
when the money dries up, the game is over

> Cicero telling us literally "unlimited money is the sinews of
> war." As well as of most other human undertakings. (See also
> VECTIGALIA NERVI SUNT REI PUBLICAE.)

nervus probandi
NEHR-wuus praw-BAHN-dee
the chief argument

> Literally "the sinew of proof."

nescis quid serus vesper ferat
NEH-skihs kwid SAY-ruus WES-pehr FEH-raht
you don't know what the night may bring

nescit plebs ieiuna (or jejuna) timere
NEH-skit playbs yay-UUN-ah tih-MAY-reh
ripe for revolution

Literally "a hungry populace knows no fear."

nescit vox missa reverti
NEH-skit wawks MIHS-sah reh-WEHR-tee
think twice before sounding off

Horace telling us literally "a word once uttered cannot be turned back."

nihil ad rem
NIH-hil ahd rem
irrelevant

Literally "nothing to do with the matter."

nihil amori iniuriam (or injuriam) est
NIH-hil ah-MOH-ree in-YUU-rih-ahm est
there is nothing that love will not forgive

Except forgetting to dry the dishes and take out the garbage.

nil conscire sibi, nulla pallescere culpa
neel kohn-SKEE-reh SIH-bih NUUL-lah pahl-LEH-skeh-reh KUUL-pah
to be able to sleep at night

Horace telling us how good it feels literally "to have a clear conscience and not pale at any charge."

nil debet
neel DAY-bet
he owes nothing

nil dictum quod non dictum prius
neel DIH-ktuum kwawd nohn DIH-ktuum PREE-uus
how hard it is to be original

Literally "nothing has been said that has not been said before."

nil magnum nisi bonum
neel MAH-gnuum NIH-sih BAW-nuum
nothing is great unless (it's) good

Not evil, that is.

nil mortalibus arduum est
neel mawr-TAH-lih-buus AHR-duu-uum est
nothing is (too) difficult for human beings

nil sine magno vita labore debit mortalibus
neel SIH-neh MAH-gnoh WEE-tah lah-BOH-reh DAY-bit mawr-TAH-lih-buus
no pain, no gain

Horace telling us literally that "life has given nothing to mankind without great labor."

nitimur in vetitum semper, cupimusque negata
NEE-tih-muur in WEH-tih-tuum SEM-pehr kuu-pih-MUUS-kweh neh-GAH-tah
forbidden fruits are sweetest

Ovid telling us literally "we are always striving for what is forbidden, and desiring what is denied us."

nitor in adversum
NEE-tawr in ahd-WEHR-suum
I struggle against misfortune

A phrase from a resolute Ovid.

nobilitas sola est atque unique virtus

noh-BIH-lih-tahs SOH-lah est AHT-kweh OO-nih-kweh WIHR-toos

virtue is the true and only nobility

According to Juvenal. (See also STEMMATA QUID FACIUNT.)

nobis iudicibus (or judicibus)

NOH-bihs yoo-DIH-kih-buus

in our opinion

Literally "we being judges."

nocet empta dolore voluptas

NAW-ket EM-ptah daw-LOH-reh waw-LUU-ptahs

let's keep things within bounds

Horace telling us literally that "pleasures brought by pain are injurious." Could the Marquis de Sade have had it wrong?

noli irritare leones

NOH-lee ihr-rih-TAH-reh lay-OH-nehs

do not provoke the lions

Don't look for trouble.

nolo episcopari

NOH-loh eh-pih-skaw-PAH-ree

I do not choose to run

An elegant Latin phrase, translated literally as "I do not wish to be a bishop," to use when turning down an appointment or nomination for high office.

nomina stultorum parietibus haerent

NOH-mih-nah stuul-TAWR-uum pah-ree-AY-tih-buus HĪ-rent

fools' names stick to the walls (of buildings)

This saying is usually given in English as a jingle, writer unknown:

> Fools' names, like fools' faces,
> Are always found in public places.

Whether given in Latin or in English, this thought is certainly not intended as a compliment. Graffiti artists were known even in ancient Pompeii, where visitors can still see their wall scribblings.

nominis umbra
NOH-mih-nihs UUM-brah
the shadow of a name

Lucan gave us this phrase, useful for describing a person or family of bygone eminence. It appears in his observation **stat magni** (staht MAH-gnih) **nominis umbra**, "there remains the shadow of a great name."

non culpabilis
nohn kuul-PAH-bih-lihs
not guilty

A verdict exonerating a person on trial.

non datur tertium
nohn DAH-tuur TEHR-tee-uum
yes or no, nothing in between

The phrase to use, literally "no third (choice) is given," when adjuring someone to choose one or the other of two paths, two actions, two candidates, or the like.

non decet
nohn DEH-ket
it is not proper

non deficiente crumena
nohn day-fih-kee-EN-teh kroo-MAY-nah
as long as the money holds out

A phrase from Horace, literally "the purse not failing," who recognized that money counts for much. (See also ET GENUS ET FORMAM REGINA PECUNIA DONAT.)

non est fumus absque igne
nohn est FOO-muus AHB-skweh IH-gneh
there is no smoke without fire

This proverb, in English dating back to the 15th century, tells us that every rumor or slander has some basis in fact. Maybe.

non est iocus (or jocus) esse malignum
nohn est YAW-kuus ES-seh mah-LIH-gnuum
jokes that hurt aren't funny

Horace telling us literally "there is no fun where there is spite."

non ex quovis ligno Mercurius fit
nohn est KWOH-wees LIH-gnoh mehr-KUU-rih-uus feet
you can't make a silk purse out of a sow's ear

We have long been told that you cannot make something good out of something that is by nature inferior in quality, here expressed literally in Latin as "you cannot make a (statue of) Mercury out of just any log." Mercury, known primarily by modern people as the messenger of the Roman gods, was also the god of eloquence, skill, trading, and thieving. Overlooking for now Mercury's last area of responsibility, we can take it that Mercury was someone worthy of high regard. Thus, the use of any ordinary wood for a statue of Mercury would surely be seen as demeaning.

non generant aquilae columbas
nohn GEH-neh-rahnt AH-kwih-lī kaw-LUUM-bahs
eagles do not bear doves

non ministrari, sed ministrare
nohn mih-nih-STRAH-ree sed min-nih-STRAH-reh
not to be ministered to, but to minister

Motto of Wellesley College.

non multa sed multum
nohn MUUL-tah sed MUUL-tuum
what is desired is quality, not quantity

Literally "not many things, but much." (See also PAUCA SED BONA.)

non nobis solum nati sumus
nohn NOH-bihs SOH-luum NAH-tee SUU-muus
not for ourselves alone are we born

non omne licitum honestum
nohn AWM-neh LIH-kih-tuum haw-NEH-stuum
not every lawful thing is honorable

Perhaps this saying ought to be made part of the oath taken by newly installed public servants. It is not enough merely to observe the letter of the law.

non possidentem multa vocaveris recte beatum
nohn paws-sih-DEN-tuum MUUL-tah waw-kah-WEH-rihs RAYK-tay beh-AH-tuum
money isn't everything

Horace telling us literally "you cannot rightly call happy the man who possesses many things."

non progredi est regredi
nohn proh-GREH-dee est reh-GREH-dee
not to go forward is to go backward

A good motto for self-styled progressives.

non quis sed quid
nohn kwihs sed kwid
not who but what

The message is clear: don't ask who says it, examine what is being said.

non revertar insultus
nohn reh-WEHR-tahr in-SUUL-tuus
I shall not return unavenged

A bold and resolute assertion by an ancient military commander who meant he would not return home without having avenged a prior defeat. In modern history, Douglas MacArthur asserted to his Filipino allies, "I shall return." Implicit in this statement was a vow to fight on to victory, and thus avenge his ignominious earlier defeat in defending the Philippine Islands.

non scribit cuius carmina nemo legit
nohn SKREE-bit KOO-yuus KAHR-mih-nah NAY-moh LEH-git
when a tree falls unheard in a forest

Martial passing a sad judgment on readers if not on writers, literally "he is no writer whose verses no one reads." Maybe he's just a bad writer.

non sibi sed patriae
nohn SIH-bih sed PAH-tree-ī
not for self but for country

nostro periculo
NAW-stroh peh-REE-kuu-loh
at our own risk

> See also MEO PERICULO.

notabilia
noh-tah-BIH-lee-ah
things worthy of note

> See also NOTATU DIGNUM.

notandum
noh-TAHN-duum
a memorandum

> Literally "something to be noted."

notatu dignum
noh-TAH-too DIH-gnuum
worthy of note

> See also NOTABILIA.

novus rex, nova lex
NAW-wuus rayks NAW-wah layks
it's a new ball game every time

Literally "new king, new law." This adage had greater currency in past times, when wars of conquest seemed to be a popular sport and nations frequently found themselves falling under foreign rule. Each time a new ruler took over the reins of government, he called the shots. Of course, the sport is by no means archaic.

noxiae poena par esto
NAW-ksih-ī POY-nah pahr EH-stoh
let the punishment match the offense

Cicero proposing that punishment for a crime be made appropriate to the severity of the crime. (See also CULPAE POENA PAR ESTO.)

nuda veritas
NOO-dah WAY-rih-tahs
naked truth

Horace gave us this phrase, also translated as "undisguised truth *or* unvarnished truth."

nudis oculis
NOO-dihs AW-kuu-lees
with the naked eyes

Without a telescope, microscope, or the like, that is.

nudis verbis
NOO-dihs WEHR-bees
in plain words

nugae canorae
NOO-gī kah-NOH-rī
melodious trifles

A condemnation.

nugae litterariae
NOO-gī liht-teh-RAH-rih-ī
literary trifles

A condemnation.

nugis addere pondus
NOO-gihs AHD-deh-reh PAWN-duus
to try to make something out of nothing

A phrase from Horace, literally "to add weight to trifles."

nulla regula sine exceptione
NUUL-lah RAY-guu-lah SIH-neh eks-keh-ptee-OH-neh
no rule without an exception

nulli desperandum quamdiu spirat
NUUL-lee deh-speh-RAHN-duum KWAHM-dyoo SPEE-raht
while there's life there's hope

Literally "no one is to be despaired of so long as he breathes." Without an artificial respirator? Also expressed as **dum spiro spero** (duum SPEE-roh SPAY-roh, "while I breathe, I hope"), a motto of South Carolina.

nulli sapere casu obtigit
NUUL-lee SAH-peh-reh KAH-suu awb-TIH-geet
people are struck dumb but never struck wise

Seneca telling us literally that "no one ever became wise by chance." It takes many years and the right natural endowment to become wise.

nullius addictus iurare (or jurare) in verba magistri
NUUL-lee-uus ahd-DIH-ktuus yoo-RAH-reh in WEHR-bah mah-GIH-stree
his own man

Horace characterizing his own sense of independence, literally "not bound to swear to the words of any master."

nunc vino pellite curas
nuunk WEE-noh PEHL-lih-teh KOO-rahs
now banish cares with wine

Horace offering advice for those who are heavily burdened. (See also ERGO BIBAMUS.)

nunquam dormio
NUUN-kwahm DAWR-mee-oh
I am ever vigilant

Literally "I never sleep."

O

obscuris vera involvens
awb-SKOO-rihs WAY-rah in-WAWL-wehns
shrouding truth in obscurity

Virgil's phrase defining the uncommon word "obfuscation," a common technique practiced by uncommonly clever people intent on confusing voters, listeners, or readers. (See also VERITAS NIHIL VERETUR NISI ABSCONDI.)

obsequium amicos, veritas odium parit
awb-SEH-kwee-uum ah-MEE-kohs WAY-rih-tahs AW-dee-uum PAH-rit
compliance breeds friends, truth hatred

ob turpem causam
awb TUUR-pem KOW-sahm
for a base cause

ob vitae solatium
awb WEE-tī soh-LAH-tih-uum
for comfort or pleasure

Literally "for the solace of life."

occasio furem facit
awk-KAH-sih-oh FOO-rem FAH-kit
don't forget to lock your car

Literally "opportunity makes the thief."

odi memorem compotorem
OH-dee MEH-maw-rem kawm-poh-TOH-rem
I hate a drinking friend with a memory

Recognition that we are apt to speak imprudently while under the influence.

odor lucri
AW-dawr LUU-kree
expectation of gain

Literally "the smell of wealth." (See also LUCRI BONUS EST ODOR.)

O fortunatos nimium, sua si bona norint!
oh fawr-too-NAH-taws NIH-mih-uum SOO-ah see BAW-nah NOH-rint
count your blessings

Virgil had farmers in mind when he said, "O too happy they, if they but knew their blessings!" and giving many of the rest of us something to think about.

O imitatores, servum pecus!
oh ih-mih-tah-TOH-rehs SEHR-wuum PEH-kuus
O imitators, you slavish herd!

Horace's phrase, especially useful in literary discussions. (See also IMITATORES, SERVUM PECUS.)

ollae amicitia
AWL-lī ah-mee-KIH-tee-ah
cupboard love

Literally translated as "friendship of the pot." Cupboard love is affection insincerely professed or displayed to obtain a favor. Narrowly defined, cupboard love is cozying up to a cook in the expectation of obtaining special or generous servings of food.

olla male fervet
AWL-lah MAH-leh FEHR-wet

the affair is going badly

Another culinary metaphor, literally "the pot boils badly," used to characterize disintegrating affairs of daily life, whether commercial or amorous. (See OLLAE AMICITIA.)

omen faustum
OH-men FOW-stuum

an auspicious omen *or* an inauspicious sign

O mihi praeteritos referat si Iuppiter (or Juppiter) annos
oh MIH-hih prī-TEH-rih-taws reh-FEH-raht see YUUP-pih-tehr AHN-naws

would that I were young again

A wistful Virgil looking back with regret: "O that Jupiter would give me back the years that are past."

omne solum forti patria est
AWM-neh SAW-luum FAWR-tee PAH-trih-ah est

to a brave man every land is his fatherland

A brave person is willing to go anywhere, even to a strange land.

omne vitium in proclivi est
AWM-neh WIH-tih-uum in praw-KLEE-wih est

one misstep leads to another

This caution tells us literally that "every vice is downhill." Also expressed as **facilis descensus Averno** (FAH-kih-lis deh-SKEN-suus ah-WEHR-noh), "the descent to hell is easy." **Avernus** was the entrance to the lower world, or the lower world itself. (See also HAEC NUGAE IN SERIA DUCENT MALA and PRINCIPIIS OBSTA.)

omnia bona bonis
AWM-nee-ah BAW-nah BAW-nees
be good but don't be naive

This observation, literally "to the good, all things are good," decries credulity.

omnia mea mecum porto
AWM-nee-ah MAY-ah MAY-kuum PAWR-toh
I scorn earthly goods

Literally "I carry with me everything that is mine." The intent here is not to glorify the backpack, but to plug frugality.

omnia mors aequat
AWM-nee-ah mawrs Ī-kwaht
the great equalizer

Claudian telling us literally that "death levels all things."

omnia praeclara rara
AWM-nee-ah prī-KLAH-rah RAH-rah
all splendid things are rare

Cicero telling us not to expect to find in life too much that is truly outstanding.

omnia suspendens naro
AWM-nee-ah suus-PEN-dehns NAH-roh
turning up one's nose at everything

omnibus has litteras visuris
AWM-nih-buus hahs LIT-teh-rahs wee-SUUR-ihs
to whom it may concern

Literally "to all who see this document."

omnibus invideas, livide, nemo tibi
AWM-nih-buus in-WIH-deh-ahs LEE-wih-deh NAY-moh TIH-bih

envy is not an endearing attribute

Literally "you may envy everybody, envious one, but nobody envies you." (See also QUI INVIDET MINOR EST.)

omnis amans amens
AWM-nees AH-mahns AH-mayns

every lover is out of his (or her) mind

Also given as **amantes sunt amentes** (ah-MAHN-tays suunt ah-MEN-tays), "lovers are lunatics."

operae pretium est
AW-peh-rī PREH-tee-uum est

it is worthwhile

Terence telling us literally "there is reward for the work"; that is, the work is worth doing.

operose nihil agunt
aw-peh-ROH-say NIH-hil AH-guunt

they are doing nothing busily

Seneca's observation of time-wasters, who are not trying to work and are fooling no one but themselves. (See also OTIOSA SEDULITAS.)

opposuit natura
awp-PAW-soo-eet nah-TOO-rah

it is unnatural

Also rendered as "it is contrary to nature," or literally as "nature has opposed."

optima interpres legum consuetudo

See CONSUETUDO EST OPTIMA INTERPRES LEGUM.

optimi consiliarii mortui

AW-ptih-mee kohn-sih-lih-AH-rih-ee MAWR-too-ee

learn from the past

Literally "the best counselors are the dead." We ignore ancient wisdom at our own peril.

optimum obsonium labor

AW-ptih-muum awb-SOH-nih-uum LAH-bawr

work is the best appetizer

More literally "work is the best means of getting a meal." And the New Testament tells us, "If any would not work, neither should he eat." Of special interest in the Latin phrase is the word *obsonium*, which is defined as "food, usually fish, eaten with bread." Thus, it can be thought of as an hors d'oeuvre, from the French, literally "outside the work." What goes around, comes around.

opum furiata cupido

AW-puum fuu-ree-AH-tah KUU-pih-doh

a frenzied lust for wealth

Ovid's phrase for the motivation that drives too many of us.

opus opificem probat

AW-puus aw-PIH-fih-kem PRAW-baht

the work proves the craftsperson

This maxim need not be applied exclusively to the traditional crafts. It's what we accomplish in any field that counts, not the glorified appellation we claim for our profession.

orate, fratres
oh-RAH-tay FRAH-trehs
pray, brothers

ore rotundo
OH-reh roh-TUUN-daw
with well-turned speech

Horace describing the smooth delivery of a fine orator, literally "with a round mouth."

ossa atque pellis totus est
AWS-sah AHT-kweh PEL-lihs TOH-tuus est
he is all skin and bones

Plautus giving us what has become and remained a vivid English cliché for the noun "emaciation."

O ter quaterque beatus!
oh tehr KWAH-tehr-kweh beh-AH-tuus
O thrice and four times blessed!

A happy phrase from Virgil.

otia dant vitia
OH-tee-ah dahnt WIH-tee-ah
the devil finds work for idle hands

Literally "leisure begets vices."

otiosa sedulitas
oh-tee-OH-sah say-DUU-lih-tahs
idle assiduity

This oxymoron suggests that some of us are capable of laborious trifling—busy work. Not true of most of us. (See also OPEROSE NIHIL AGUNT and STRENUA INERTIA.)

otium sine dignitate
OH-tee-uum SIH-neh dih-gnih-TAH-teh
leisure without dignity

The opposite of **otium cum** (kuum) **dignitate**, "leisure with dignity."

otium sine litteris mors est
OH-tee-uum SIH-neh LIT-teh-rees mawrs est
take books along next summer

Seneca telling us "leisure without literature is death." The phrase *sine litteris* can also be translated as "uncultured," but we would not say "uncultured leisure."

P

pabulum animi
PAH-buu-luum AH-nih-mee
learning

Literally "food for the mind."

pacta conventa
PAH-ktah kawn-WEN-tah
a diplomatic pact

Literally "the conditions agreed upon."

pactum illicitum
PAH-ktuum il-LIH-kih-tuum
an unlawful agreement

pallidus ira
PAHL-lih-duus EE-rah
pale with rage

palmam qui meruit ferat
PAHL-mahm kwee MEH-ruu-eet FEH-raht

may the best man win

The motto, literally "let him bear the palm who has deserved it," of Lord Nelson (1758-1805), the great British admiral. In ancient Rome, a victorious gladiator was given a branch of the palm tree. Thus "bear the palm" means "be the best."

palma non sine pulvere
PAHL-mah nohn SIH-neh PUUL-weh-reh

no gain without pain

A Roman proverb, literally "the palm not without effort," telling us that no one achieves success without struggle. For another meaning of **pulvis** (PUUL-wihs), the nominative form of the ablative *pulvere*, see PULVIS ET UMBRA SUMUS. (See also PALMAM QUI MERUIT FERAT for the significance of "palm.")

par bene comparatum
pahr BEH-neh kawm-pah-RAH-tuum

a well-matched pair

parce, parce, precor
PAHR-keh PAHR-keh PREH-kawr

spare me, spare me, I pray

parcere subiectis (or subjectis) et debellare superbos
PAHR-keh-reh suub-YEH-ktihs et day-behl-LAH-reh SUU-pehr-baws

to spare the vanquished and subdue the proud

Virgil explaining the balanced aim of Roman conquest.

parem non feret
PAH-rem nohn FEH-ret
he (or she) brooks no equal

The mind-set of the egocentric person.

paritur pax bello
PAH-rih-tuur pahks BEL-loh
peace is born of war

See also ARMA TUENTUR PACEM.

par negotiis neque supra
pahr neh-GOH-tih-ees NEH-kweh SUU-prah
vocational bliss

Literally "equal to work and not above it." Tacitus describing a person well suited to his or her occupation.

par oneri
pahr AW-neh-ree
equal to the burden

pars pro toto
pahrs proh TOH-toh
synecdoche

Literally "a part for the whole." Saying "we need new faces" rather than "we need new employees" is an example of synecdoche—the rhetorical use of a part to represent the whole.

pars sanitatis velle sanari fuit
pahrs sah-nih-TAH-tihs WEL-leh sah-NAH-ree FOO-eet
to be cured one must wish to be cured

An insight from Seneca remarkable for its time, literally "part of health is to want to be healed."

parva componere magnis
PAHR-wah kawm-POH-neh-reh MAH-gnihs
to compare small things with great

parvis componere magna
PAHR-wihs kawm-POH-neh-reh MAH-gnah
to compare great things with small

parvis e glandibus quercus
PAHR-wihs ay GLAHN-dih-buus KWEHR-kuus
the mighty oak from little acorns grows

Great things have small beginnings. (See also GUTTA CAVAT LAPIDEM, CONSUMITUR ANULUS USU.)

parvum parva decent
PAHR-wuum PAHR-wah DEH-kent
small things befit the humble person

An adage from Horace implying that great things befit the proud or ambitious person.

patres conscripti
PAH-trehs kohn-SKREE-ptee
legislators

Literally "the conscript fathers," by definition the patrician and the elected plebeian members of the ancient Roman Senate. The phrase derives from the enrollment of senators by Junius Brutus (85–42 B.C.), the first Roman consul.

patria cara, carior libertas
PAH-trih-ah KAH-rah KAH-ree-awr lee-BEHR-tahs
my native land is dear, but liberty is dearer

patriae infelici fidelis
PAH-trih-ī een-fay-LEE-kih fih-DAY-lihs
faithful to my unhappy country

patria potestas
PAH-trih-ah paw-TEHS-tahs
parental authority

A legal term for the power of a Roman father over his family, a power not inconsiderable when compared with the role of the modern father in most parts of the world. At one time a Roman father even had power of life and limb over his wife and children.

pauca sed bona
POW-kah sed BAW-nah
not quantity but quality

A motto, literally "a few things but good," often given as "less is more." (See also NON MULTA SED MULTUM.)

paucis verbis
POW-kees WEHR-bees
in few words

paulo maiora canamus
POW-loh mī-OH-rah kah-NAH-muus
let us sing of somewhat loftier things

From Virgil, who sang of loftier things.

paulum morati, serius aut citius sedem properamus ad unum
POW-luum maw-RAH-tee SAY-rih-uus owt KIH-tih-uus
SAY-dem praw-pehr-AH-muus ahd OO-nuum
we all must die one day

Ovid on the inevitability of death, literally "after a slight delay, sooner or later we hasten to one and the same abode." (See what Horace had to say on this subject in PULVIS ET UMBRA SUMUS.)

pectus est quod disertos facit
PEH-ktuus est kwawd dih-SEHR-taws FAH-kit
speak from the heart

Quintilian telling us how to become successful orators, literally "it is the heart that makes persons eloquent." So when you speak from the heart, the words will take care of themselves. We hope. (See also REM TENE ET VERBA SEQUENTUR.)

pedibus timor addidit alas
PEH-dih-buus TIH-mawr AHD-dih-deet AH-lahs
a good scare can turn you into an Olympic sprinter

An adage from Virgil, literally "fear has added wings to one's feet."

Pelio imponere Ossam
PAY-lee-oh im-POH-neh-reh AWS-sahm
to pile hardship upon hardship

Literally "to pile Pelion upon Ossa," but also freely rendered in English as "to pile embarrassment upon embarrassment." Pelion and Ossa are both mountain peaks in Thessaly. In the *Odyssey*, when the giants wanted to climb to heaven and destroy the gods, they lifted up Pelion and placed it atop Ossa. Incidentally, Ossa was the home of the centaurs.

per aetatem
pehr ī-TAH-tem
by reason of one's age

per aevum
pehr Ī-wuum
forever

> Literally "for eternity."

per ambages
pehr ahm-BAH-gays
beating around the bush

> This phrase can be rendered literally as "by windings," more felicitously as "by circumlocution" or "by quibbling."

per aspera ad astra
pehr AH-speh-rah ahd AH-strah
through difficulties to the stars

> Also given as **ad astra per aspera**, the motto of Kansas. Either way, this well-known saying has nothing to do with the Hubble Space Telescope, but teaches that we achieve great things only by encountering and overcoming adversity.

percontatorem fugito, nam garrulus idem est
pehr-kawn-tah-TOH-rem FUU-gih-toh nahm GAHR-ruu-luus EE-dem est
watch out for snoopers

> Horace providing a worthwhile proverb, literally "shun an inquisitive man, for he is sure to be a gossip."

pereunt et imputantur
PEH-reh-uunt et eem-puu-TAHN-tuur
how time passes

> A sundial inscription, almost literally "they (the hours or years) pass away and are charged to one's account."

per gradus
pehr GRAH-duus
step by step

periculum fortitudine evasi
peh-REE-kuu-luum fawr-tih-TOO-dih-neh ay-WAH-see
by courage I have escaped danger

> Others have succeeded by less audacious means.

per iocum (or jocum)
pehr YAW-kuum
for fun

> Also rendered as "in jest" and "by way of a joke."

peritis in sua arte credendum
peh-REE-tihs in SOO-ah AHR-teh kray-DEN-duum
watch out for the know-it-all

> Literally "the experts should be trusted in their own areas of competence." But not outside them.

per legem terrae
pehr LAY-gehm TEHR-rī
by the law of the land

pernicibus alis
pehr-NEE-kih-buus AH-lihs
rapidly

> Virgil's phrase, literally "with swift wings."

per pares
pehr PAH-rays
by one's peers

perpetuum mobile
pehr-PEH-too-uum MOH-bih-leh
perpetual motion

More accurately rendered as "something perpetually in motion."

per saltum
pehr SAHL-tuum
by a leap

This phrase may also be rendered as "without intermediate stages" or "skipping over intermediate stages."

per tot discrimina rerum
pehr tawt dih-SKREE-mih-nah RAY-ruum
through so many critical moments

Virgil's phrase.

pia desideria
PEE-ah day-see-DEH-ree-ah
pious regrets

pia fraus
PEE-ah frows
a pious fraud

Ovid's phrase. Also given as FRAUS PIA.

piscem natare doces
PIH-skem nah-TAH-reh DAW-kehs
you are wasting your time

Literally "you are teaching a fish to swim," also rendered traditionally as "you're carrying coals to Newcastle." (See also IN SILVAM LIGNA FERRE.)

pleno iure (or jure)
PLAY-noh YOO-reh
with full authority

plus in posse quam in actu
ploos in PAWS-seh kwahm in AHK-too
more in possibility than in fact

Useful in suggesting that something described as existing may not really exist at all.

plus minusve
ploos MIH-nuus-weh
more or less

poesis est vinum daemonium
paw-AY-sihs est WEE-nuum dī-MOH-nih-uum
poetry is devil's wine

A powerful literary form is poetry, with the ability to besot comparable to that of wine.

populus me sibilat, at mihi plaudo
PAW-puu-luus may SEE-bih-laht aht MIH-hih PLOW-doh
who cares what people say?

Horace, who did not quake when facing rejection, telling us literally "the people hiss me, but I applaud myself." Like the advice given by Shakespeare's Polonius, "This above all—to thine own self be true," a motto for all who have faith in themselves.

posse videor
PAWS-seh WIH-deh-awr
I seem to be able

A phrase that may be taken as anticipating the mantra "I think I can, I think I can," of *The Little Engine That Could.*

post bellum auxilium
pawst BEL-luum owk-SIH-lih-uum
where were you when I needed you?

A sad phrase, literally "help after the war," for help that comes too late. Bosnia, Rwanda, Somalia, Sudan. . .

post factum nullum consilium
pawst FAH-ktuum NUUL-lum kohn-SIH-lee-uum
now yóu tell me!

Literally "after the deed, no advice is helpful."

post litem motam
pawst LEE-tem MOH-tahm
after litigation began

A phrase in law.

post obitum
pawst AW-bih-tuum
after death

post prandium
pawst PRAHN-dee-uum
after a meal

post proelia praemia
pawst PROY-lee-ah PRĪ-mih-ah
after battles, rewards

For the victors, that is.

post tenebras lux
pawst TEH-neh-brahs luuks
after darkness, light

> After despair, news bringing hope.

potior est conditio possidentis
PAW-tee-awr est kawn-DEE-tih-oh paws-sih-DEN-tihs
possession is nine points of the law

> Literally "the possessor is in a better condition."

praemia virtutis
PRĪ-mih-ah wihr-TOO-tihs
the rewards of virtue

praemissis praemittendis
prī-MIS-sihs prī-mit-TEN-dihs
getting to the point

> Literally "omitting preliminaries."

praesto et persto
PRĪ-stoh et PEHR-stoh
I stand in front and I stand fast

> The attitude of the valiant leader, willing to expose himself or herself to attack and never retreat.

praeteriti anni
prī-TEH-rih-tee AHN-nee
bygone years

pretio parata vincitur pretio fides
PREH-tee-oh pah-RAH-tah WIN-kih-tuur PREH-tee-oh
FIH-days
loyalty isn't for sale

This proverb, literally "loyalty gained through bribes is lost through bribes," warns against trying to buy friendship.

prima caritas incipit a se ipso
PREE-mah KAH-rih-tahs in-KIH-pit ah say IH-psoh
charity begins at home

> Literally "charity begins first with oneself."

primo intuiti
PREE-moh in-TOO-ih-tee
at first glance

primo mihi
PREE-moh MIH-hih
for myself first

primum non nocere
PREE-muum nohn NAW-keh-reh
first of all, do no harm

A medical aphorism adjuring the physician to avoid employing a remedy that is worse than the disease to be cured.

principia, non homines
preen-KIH-pee-ah nohn HAW-mih-nays
the rule of law, not the rule of men

> Literally "principles, not men."

principibus placuisse viris non ultima laus est
preen-KIH-pih-buus plah-kuu-EES-seh WIH-rees nohn UUL-tih-mah lows est
the best praise is that given by qualified critics

Horace, who had his share of recognition, telling us literally "to have won the approbation of eminent men is not the
lowest praise."

principiis obsta
preen-KIH-pih-ees AWB-stah
resist the beginnings

It's the first misstep that counts, and the first indiscretion
leads inevitably to more. (See also HAEC NUGAE IN SERIA DUCUNT
MALA and OMNE VITIUM IN PROCLIVI EST.)

prior tempore, prior iure (or jure)
PREE-awr TEM-paw-reh PREE-awr YOO-reh
first come, first served

Literally "first in time, first by right."

pristinae virtutis memores
PREE-stih-nī wihr-TOO-tihs MEH-maw-rehs
mindful of the valor of former days

Everything was better in the old days.

probitas verus honor
PRAW-bih-tahs WAY-ruus HAW-nawr
honesty is true honor

Because it takes courage to be completely honest.

prodesse quam conspici
proh-DES-seh kwahm KOHN-spih-kee
to be of service rather than to be gazed at

The reason why the best of us do our best.

pro et contra
proh et KAWN-trah
for and against

pro forma tantum
proh FAWR-mah TAHN-tuum
for form only

>   Just for appearances.

pro libertate patriae
proh lee-behr-TAH-teh PAH-trih-ī
for the liberty of my country

pro nunc
proh nuunk
for now

proprio iure (or **jure**)
PRAW-pree-oh YOO-reh
in one's own right

proprio vigore
PRAW-pree-oh wih-GOH-reh
independently

>   Literally "of one's own strength" or "by its own force."

pro pudor!
proh PUU-dawr
for shame!

pro virili parte
proh WIH-rih-lee PAHR-teh
to the best of one's ability

>   All one can ask of anyone.

pro virtute felix temeritas
proh wihr-TOO-teh FAY-leeks teh-MEH-rih-tahs
in place of courage a lucky foolhardiness

Beats cowardice.

pugnis et calcibus
PUU-gnees et KAHL-kih-buus
tooth and nail

To win in an important struggle, you are well advised to go at it with all you have, literally "with fists and heels."

pulvis et umbra sumus
PUUL-wihs et UUM-brah SUUM-uus
in the end we are nothing

Horace, in a poignant reminder of our mortality, telling us literally "we are but dust and shadow." (For Ovid on death, see PAULUM MORATI, SERIUS AUT CITIUS SEDEM PROPERAMUS AD UNUM.)

Q

quae amissa salva
kwī ah-MIHS-sah SAHL-wah
things lost are safe

Perhaps in the sense that they cannot be lost a second time.

quae e longinquo magis placent
kwī ay lawn-GIHN-kwoh MAH-gihs PLAH-kent
distance lends enchantment

Literally "things from afar please the more." Two other phrases are often seen that convey the same meaning: **maior e longinquo reverentia** (MAH-yawr ay lawn-GIHN-kwoh reh-weh-REN-tee-ah, "greater reverence from afar") and **omne ignotum pro magnifico est** (AWM-neh ih-GNOH-tuum proh mah-GNIH-fih-koh est, "everything unknown is thought magnificent").

quae fuerunt vitia mores sunt
kwī FOO-eh-ruunt WIH-tih-ah MOH-rehs suunt
what once were vices now are customs

Seneca commenting on what he perceived as a decline in public values. Cole Porter observed the same decline, but with characteristic jocularity gave us "now, goodness knows, anything goes."

quae non valeant singula iuncta (or juncta) iuvant (or juvant)
kwī nohn WAH-lay-ahnt SIN-guu-lah YUUN-ktah YUU-wahnt
united we stand, divided we fall

Literally "things that do not avail singly are effective when united."

quaestio vexata
KWĪ-stih-oh weh-KSAH-tah
a vexed *or* distressing question

A question that touches on sensitive matters or a disputed question. Also given as VEXATA QUAESTIO.

qualis rex, talis grex
KWAH-lihs rayks TAH-lihs greks
as the shepherd, so the flock

The Latin phrase speaks of a king (*rex*) and a flock (*grex*), making some editors unhappy because of what they perceive as a mixed metaphor, but the phrase in its entirety is in common use to convey the meaning that the nature of a people is largely determined by the nature of its leadership. And we are left with the inference that *qualis rex, talis grex*, literally "as the king, so the flock," can be applied to other types of organizations, including sports teams and businesses.

qualis vir, talis oratio
KWAH-lihs wihr TAH-lihs oh-RAH-tee-oh
as the man, so the speech

So maybe words do not always make the man. Here we are told that the opposite claim can also be valid.

qualis vita, finis ita
KWAH-lihs WEE-tah FEE-nihs IH-tah
as the life, so the death

The word *finis* can, of course, also be translated as "end," with the thought remaining the same—a good life ends in a good way, a bad life in an end less satisfactory.

quamdiu se bene gesserit
KWAHM-dih-oo say BEH-neh GEHS-seh-reet
during good behavior

Parolees and students should keep this phrase in mind as a requirement for continuing privileges. Its literal translation is "as long as he (or she) behaves well."

quam parva sapientia mundus regitur!
kwahm PAHR-wah sah-pih-EN-tih-ah MUUN-duus REH-gih-tuur
with how little wisdom the world is governed!

And things are not getting any better.

quam primum
kwahm PREE-muum
as soon as possible

If not immediately or forthwith, both of which adverbs can be used as translations of *quam primum*.

quam proxime
kwahm PRAW-ksih-may
as nearly as possible

quanti est sapere!
KWAHN-tee est SAH-peh-reh
how grand it is to be wise!

A phrase from Terence that can be used literally or sardonically.

quantum mutatis ab illo!
KWAHN-tuum moo-TAH-tihs ahb IL-loh
how much changed from the man he was!

Virgil giving us the phrase of choice for gossiping about a person who has become altered in appearance or character.

quasi dictum
KWAH-sih DIH-ktuum
as if said

quasi dixisset
KWAH-sih dik-SIHS-set
as if he (or she) had said

quem Iuppiter (or Juppiter) vult perdere, prius dementat
kwem YUUP-pih-tehr wuult PEHR-deh-reh PREE-uus deh-MEN-taht
whom Jupiter wishes to destroy, he first makes mad

So that he will destroy himself.

qui capit ille facit
kwee KAH-pit IL-leh FAH-kit
if the shoe fits, wear it

Literally "he who takes it (a disparaging remark) on himself has done it."

quicquid praecipies esto brevis
KWIK-kwid prī-KIH-pih-ehs EH-stoh BREH-wihs
keep it short

Horace giving us a valid lesson in rhetoric, literally "whatever you're trying to teach us, be brief."

quid caeco cum speculo?
kwid KĪ-koh kuum SPEH-kuu-loh
why a blind person with a mirror?

A way to voice suspicion when confronted by an incongruous situation.

qui dedit beneficium taceat; narret qui accepit
kwee DAY-dit beh-neh-FIH-kih-uum TAH-keh-aht NAHR-ret kwee ahk-KAY-peet
don't boast about your acts of charity

Seneca telling us not to embarrass a person we help, literally "let the person who performed the kind act keep silent; let the recipient tell about it."

quid hoc sibi vult?
kwid hohk SIH-bih wuult
what does this mean?

quid leges sine moribus vanae proficiunt?
kwid LAY-gehs SIH-neh MOH-rih-buus WAH-nī proh-FIH-kih-uunt
you can't legislate morality

Literally "of what use are idle laws in the absence of morals?"

quid non mortalia pectora cogis, auri sacra fames?
kwid nohn mawr-TAH-lee-ah PEK-taw-rah KOH-gihs OW-ree SAH-krah FAH-mays

greed, greed, greed

Virgil, who knew better than to fall victim to greed, declaiming literally "to what do you not drive the hearts of men, accursed hunger for gold?"

quid prodest?
kwid PROH-dest

what good does it do?

quidquid delirant reges, plectuntur Achivi
KWID-kwid day-LEE-rahnt RAY-gehs plek-TUUN-tuur ah-KEE-wee

whatever folly their rulers commit, the Greeks suffer the penalty

A proverb of Horace that has not lost its cogency over the centuries, suggesting that it's the innocent people who get hurt. **Achivus** (ah-KEE-wuus) was an ancient name for "Greek." Today, in place of "Greeks" read "Bosnians," "Haitians," or any of a multiplicity of other peoples.

quid rides?
kwid REE-dehs

why are you laughing?

quid sit futurum cras, fuge quaerere
kwid sit fuu-TOO-ruum krahs FUU-geh KWĪ-reh-reh

live in the here and now

Horace advising us literally to "avoid asking what tomorrow will bring." Nobody will know until tomorrow is today.

quid times?
kwid TIH-mehs
what do you fear?

quid verum atque decens
kwid WAY-ruum AHT-kweh DEH-kayns
what is true and seemly

Television executives and newscasters, consider this phrase from Horace when planning your programs.

quieta non movere
kwee-AY-tah nohn moh-WAY-reh
let sleeping dogs lie

Literally "not to disturb quiet things," better translated as "don't disturb things that are at peace." Today some of us are apt to say, "If it ain't broke, don't fix it." (See also NE PRIUS ANTIDOTUM QUAM VENENAM.)

qui facit per alium facit per se
kwee FAH-kit pehr AH-lee-uum FAH-kit pehr say
you cannot shift the blame

This legal principle, literally "he who does a thing through another does it himself," tells us that we are legally responsible for the actions of our agents. So if someone you hire steals a car for you, you can expect to be charged with the theft yourself.

qui iacet (or jacet) in terra non habet unde cadat
kwee YAH-ket in TEHR-rah nohn HAH-bet UUN-deh KAH-daht
nowhere to go but up

This observation, literally "he who lies on the ground has no chance to fall," puts the best face on a desperate situation. John Bunyan, the 17th-century English writer and preacher whose pilgrim made considerable progress, put it this way: "He that is down, needs fear no fall."

qui invidet minor est
kwee in-WIH-det MIH-nawr est
he who envies is the less for it

> See also OMNIBUS INVIDEAS, LIVIDE, NEMO TIBI.

qui male agit odit lucem
kwee MAH-leh AH-git OH-deet LOO-kem
he who does evil hates daylight

> And that's why malefactors shudder at the thought of sunshine laws. (See also EX UMBRA IN SOLEM.)

qui nimium probat nihil probat
kwee NIH-mih-uum PROH-baht NIH-hil PROH-baht
he who proves too much proves nothing

Stay with the central point you are trying to make. Don't answer questions you have not been asked. And, for the trial lawyer, don't ask an idle question. You don't know what damaging information will be revealed in the answer.

qui non proficit deficit
kwee nohn proh-FIH-kit day-FIH-kit
it's pointless to run in place

More literally "he (or she) who does not advance loses ground." This would appear to be the guiding principle of aggressive entrepreneurs. By putting too much faith in this dictum and trying to grow too fast, they may endanger an already successful enterprise.

qui parcit nocentibus innocentes punit
kwee PAHR-kit noh-KEN-tih-buus in-naw-KAYN-tehs POO-nit
an argument for harsh justice

Literally "who spares the guilty punishes the innocent." (For another way of saying the same thing, see BONIS NOCET QUISQUIS PEPERCERIT MALIS.)

qui sentit commodum sentire debet et onus
kwee SEN-tit KAWM-maw-duum sen-TEE-reh DAY-bet et AW-nuus
there's no free lunch

Literally "he (or she) who experiences the benefit should experience the burden as well."

quocumque modo
kwoh-KUUM-kweh MAW-doh
in whatever manner

quocumque nomine
kwoh-KUUM-kweh NOH-mih-neh
under whatever name

quod absurdum est
kwawd ahb-SUUR-duum est
which thing is absurd

A phrase used to close an argument based on demonstrating that an opponent's argument cannot logically be true.

quod bene notandum
kwawd BEH-neh noh-TAHN-duum
which is to be especially noted

A scholarly notation.

quod bonum, felix, faustumque sit!
kwawd BAW-nuum FAY-leeks FOW-stuum-kweh sit
and may it be lucky, prosperous, and auspicious!

Could anyone ask for more? An excellent candidate for inclusion in a toast offered at a wedding celebration.

quod licet Iovi (or Jovi) non licet bovi
kwawd LIH-ket YAW-wee nohn LIH-ket BOH-wee
that which Jove is permitted, an ox is not

Except perhaps for citizens of perfect democracies, we are not all entitled to the same treatment in all matters—Jove was an alternative name for Jupiter, and Jupiter was a very important god. An ox is an ox.

quod minime crederes
kwawd MIH-nih-may KRAY-deh-rays
what one would least suppose

quod non opus est, asse carum est
kwawd nohn AW-puus est AHS-seh KAH-ruum est
what is not necessary is dear at a penny

Good to keep in mind when shopping a sale or making one's way through a flea market.

quod sciam
kwawd SKEE-ahm
as far as I know

quod sentimus loquamur, quod loquimur sentiamus
kwawd SEN-tih-muus LAW-kwah-muur kwawd LAW-kwih-muur sen-tih-AH-muus
say what you mean, mean what you say

A maxim from Seneca, literally "let us say what we think, let us understand what we say." For those who study each word in this entry, understand that the verb **sentio** (SEN-tih-oh), of which *sentimus* and *sentiamus* are forms, has many meanings.

quod volumus, facile credimus
kwawd WOH-luu-muus FAH-kih-leh KRAY-dih-muus
we readily believe what we wish to believe

quo fas et gloria ducunt
kwoh fahs et GLOH-ree-ah DOO-kuunt
where duty and glory lead

quo Fata vocant
kwoh FAH-tah WAW-kahnt
whither the Fates call

The Romans were fatalistic. When we go *quo Fata vocant*, we avoid taking responsibility for our own actions.

quo pax et gloria ducunt
kwoh pahks et GLOH-ree-ah DOO-kuunt
where peace and glory lead

quorum pars magna fui
KWOH-ruum pahrs MAH-gnah FOO-ee
of which I was an important part

Aeneas, in Virgil's *Aeneid*, launching his recital to Dido of the disasters that befell the Trojans.

quot servi tot hostes
kwawt SEHR-wee tawt HAWS-tehs
watch out especially for the people close to you

Literally "so many servants, so many enemies."

quousque tandem abutere patientia nostra?
kwoh-UUS-kweh TAHN-dem ah-BUU-teh-reh pah-tee-
EN-tee-ah NAWS-trah
how long will you abuse our patience?

The famous question that Cicero, in an oration before the Roman Senate, addressed to Catiline (Lucius Sergius Catilina), who conspired to plunder the Roman treasury and destroy the Senate. (See also ALIENI APPETENS.)

R

redintegratio amoris
reh-din-teh-GRAH-tee-oh ah-MOH-rihs
the renewal of love

redire ad nuces
reh-DEE-reh ahd NUU-kehs
to resume childish follies

This expression, literally "to return to the nuts," is the opposite of **relinquere** (reh-LIN-kweh-reh) **nuces**, "to abandon the nuts." In ancient Rome it was conventional after a wedding for the bridegroom to scatter nuts to the onlookers in the street, to symbolize that he was giving up boyish playthings. Thus, *redire ad nuces* represents a regression from adulthood, much like watching football games on TV all day Sunday while one's spouse steams.

Regina Caeli
ray-GEE-nah KĪ-lee
the Virgin Mary

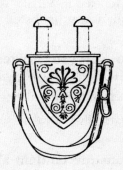

Literally "Queen of Heaven."

regium donum
RAY-gih-uum DOH-nuum
a royal grant *or* a royal gift

regnat populus
RAY-gnaht PAW-puu-luus
the people rule

Motto of Arkansas.

re infecta
ray een-FEH-ktah
unfinished business

Literally "the matter being unfinished," also translated as "without achieving one's purpose."

relata refero
reh-LAH-tah REH-feh-roh
I tell the tale as it was told to me

Don't blame me, I was only the reporter. A way to deny responsibility for an account one gives.

religio loci
ray-LIH-gee-oh LAW-kī
the sanctity of the place

reliquiae
ray-LIH-kwih-ī
the remains

Of a person who has died, that is. Also translated as "relics."

rem acu tangere
rem AH-koo TAHN-geh-reh
to hit the nail on the head

See also TETIGISTI ACU.

remisso animo
reh-MIHS-soh AH-nih-moh
listlessly

Literally "with mind relaxed."

rem tene et verba sequentur
rem TEH-neh et WEHR-bah seh-KWEN-tuur
master the material and the words will follow

See also PECTUS EST QUOD DISERTOS FACIT.

renovate animos
reh-naw-WAH-teh AH-nih-mohs
renew your courage

See also REVOCATE ANIMOS.

repente liberalis stultis gratus est; verum peritis irritos tendit dolos
reh-PEN-teh lee-beh-RAH-lihs STUUL-tihs GRAH-tuus est WAY-ruum peh-REE-tihs IHR-rih-taws TEN-dit DAW-lohs
when someone starts giving money away, look out

Wisdom from Plautus, literally "a man who is suddenly generous pleases fools, but his tricks make no impression on the experienced."

repetitio est mater studiorum
reh-peh-TEE-tih-oh est MAH-tehr stuu-dih-AW-ruum
repetition is the mother of studies

And that's why homework was born.

rerum primordia
RAY-ruum pree-MOHR-dee-ah

atoms

Literally "the first beginnings of things." The Romans followed the Greeks in seeing atoms as the smallest elements of matter. Today's physicists speak of quarks and other particles much smaller than atoms.

res adversae
rays ahd-WEHR-sī

adversity *or* adverse things

res domesticas noli tangere
rays daw-MEHS-tih-kahs NOH-lee TAHN-geh-reh

mind your own business

Literally "don't interfere in the domestic affairs of others."

res est ingeniosa dare
rays est in-geh-nee-OH-sah DAH-reh

giving requires good sense

Ovid telling us that how and when and to whom one gives are as important as the act of giving itself.

res est sacra miser
rays est SAH-krah MIH-sehr

an impoverished person is a sacred object

So be generous in giving charity.

res gestae
rays GEH-stī

facts

Also translated as "things done," "deeds," "exploits," "transactions" and, in law, "the material facts."

res incognitae
rays in-KAW-gnih-tī
things unknown *or* matters unknown

res iudicata (or judicata)
rays yoo-dih-KAH-tah
an adjudicated matter

This phrase is seen in a legal maxim: **res iudicata pro veritate accipitur** (proh way-rih-TAH-teh ahk-KIH-pih-tuur), literally "a case that has been decided is accepted as truth."

res secundae
rays seh-KUUN-dī
prosperity *or* success

Literally "favorable things."

revocate animos
reh-waw-KAH-teh AH-nih-mohs
recover your courage

See also RENOVATE ANIMOS.

rex convivii
rayks kawn-WEE-wih-ee
king of the feast *or* master of the feast

Also given as **rex bibendi** (bih-BEN-dee), literally "king of the drinking," and as **rex vini** (WEE-nee), literally "king of the wine."

rex regnat sed non gubernat
rayks RAY-gnaht sed nohn guu-BEHR-naht
a leader remiss in his duties

Literally "the king reigns but does not govern."

ridentum dicere verum quid vetat?
ree-DEN-tuum DEE-keh-reh WAY-ruum kwid WEH-taht
many a true word is said in jest

Horace asking literally "what prohibits one from speaking the truth even while laughing?"

ridere in stomacho
ree-DAY-reh in STAW-mah-koh
to laugh up one's sleeve

Literally "to laugh in the stomach *or* in the gullet."

risum teneatis, amici?
REE-suum teh-neh-AH-tihs ah-MEE-kee
can this guy be for real?

A rhetorical question from Horace, literally "could you help laughing, my friends?"

rixatur de lana saepe caprina
rih-KSAH-tuur day LAH-nah SĪ-peh kah-PREE-nah
he (or she) quarrels about nothing

Literally "he (or she) often quarrels about goat's wool." For an explanation of the significance of goat's wool, see DE LANA CAPRINA.

Roma locuta est, causa finita est
ROH-mah law-KOO-tah est KOW-sah fee-NEE-tah est
that's the end of the matter

Literally "Rome has spoken, the case is ended." The allusion is to the Vatican, or papal authority, which is taken as having the final word among Roman Catholics in any discussion of theological principles and practices.

rudis indigestaque moles
RUU-dihs in-dee-GEH-stah-kweh MOH-lays
a chaotic condition

Well translated also as "a formless mass" or more literally as "a rude and undigested mass."

S

saepe creat molles aspera spina rosas
SĪ-peh KREH-aht MAWL-lehs AH-speh-rah SPEE-nah RAW-sahs
good things from unexpected sources

Ovid in an expansive but realistic mood, telling us literally "a sharp thorn often produces delicate roses."

saeva indignatio
SĪ-wah in-dih-GNAH-tee-oh
fierce indignation

Virgil's phrase.

saevis tranquillus in undis
SĪ-wihs trahn-KWIL-luus in UUN-dihs
keeping cool when all hell is breaking loose

Literally "calm amid the raging waters." (See also AEQUAM MEMENTO REBUS IN ARDUIS SERVARE MENTEM.)

sal sapit omnia
sahl SAH-pit AWM-nee-ah
salt seasons everything

Table salt, sodium chloride, is not intended here. Rather, for "salt" read "wit" or "sparkling thought well expressed." Now *sal sapit omnia* cannot be denied. What's better, wouldn't you say, than good conversation at a meal, no matter how well or poorly prepared? The food, that is. (See also MERUM SAL.)

salva conscientia
SAHL-wah kohn-skee-EN-tih-ah
with a clear conscience

This phrase can also be translated as "without compromising one's conscience" or, literally, "with conscience intact."

salva dignitate
SAHL-wah dih-gnih-TAH-teh
without compromising one's dignity

Literally "with dignity uninjured." And that's the outcome we all hope for after we have taken a beating of one sort or another.

salva fide
SAHL-wah FIH-day
without breaking one's word

Literally "with safety to one's honor."

salva lege
SAHL-wah LAY-geh
without breaking the law

salva res est
SAHL-wah rays est
all is well

salva sit reverentia
SAHL-wah sit reh-weh-REN-tee-ah
let due respect be observed

salvo iure (or jure)
SAHL-woh YOO-reh
without prejudice

A legal term, literally "the right (of someone) being unimpaired."

salvo pudore
SAHL-woh puu-DOH-reh
without shame

salvo sensu
SAHL-woh SAYN-suu
without changing the meaning

This is the challenge faced by translators and editors, to do their work well, literally "without violation of sense."

sapere aude

See AUDE SAPERE.

sapiens dominabitur astris
SAH-pih-ayns daw-mih-NAH-bih-tuur AH-strihs
the wise man will be master of the stars

That is, he will be master of himself, free of the influence of the stars. As Shakespeare's Cassius said:

Men at some time are masters of their fates:
The fault, dear Brutus, is not in our stars,
But in ourselves, that we are underlings.

sapiens, in se ipso totus, teres atque rotundus
SAH-pih-ayns in say IH-psoh TOH-tuus TEH-rehs AHT-kweh raw-TUUN-duus
a wise man, complete in himself, well-rounded and polished

Horace describing someone admirable. How much better can one get?

sapiens qui prospicit
SAH-pih-ayns kwee PROH-spih-kit
wise is he (or she) who looks ahead

sapientem pascere barbam
sah-pih-EN-tem PAH-skeh-reh BAHR-bahm
to foster growth of the beard of the wise

The continuing preoccupation of many young men who hope that looking wise can equate with being wise.

sat cito si sat bene
saht KEE-toh see saht BEH-neh
fast enough if well enough

sat cito si sat tuto
saht KEE-toh see saht TOO-toh
fast enough if safely enough

satis quod sufficit
SAH-tihs kwawd suuf-FIH-kit
enough is as good as a feast

A plug for moderation, literally "what suffices is enough." A spoonful of caviar, not a bowlful; a slice or two of pizza, not the entire pie.

sat pulchra si sat bona
saht PUUL-krah see saht BAW-nah
handsome is as handsome does

Literally "beautiful enough if she is good enough." One's actions count for more than one's looks, they say.

scala caeli
SKAH-lah KĪ-lee
ladder to heaven *or* staircase to heaven

scelere velandum est scelus
SKEH-leh-reh weh-LAHN-duum est SKEH-luus
one misstep leads to another

Irrefutable wisdom from Seneca, literally "one crime has to be concealed by another." (For what Terence had to say along the same lines, see FALLACIA ALIA ALIAM TRUDIT.)

schola cantorum
SKAW-lah kahn-TOH-ruum
school of singers

scienter
skee-EN-tehr
expertly

While the translation above is accurate, when the term appears in a legal context a better translation is "knowingly" or "willfully."

scio cui credidi
SKEE-oh KOO-ee KRAY-dih-dee
I know whom I have trusted

The credo of the careful credit manager.

scire quid valeant humeri, quid ferre recusent
SKEE-reh kwid WAH-lay-ahnt HUU-meh-ree kwid FEHR-reh reh-KOO-sent
to know one's limitations

Literally "to know what one's shoulders can carry, what they refuse to carry." The intent here goes beyond burdens literally borne on one's shoulders to debts, demanding studies, work schedules, manuscript deadlines, and all the rest of the demands put on people all through their lives.

scribendi recte sapere est et principium et fons
skree-BEN-dee RAYK-tay SAH-peh-reh est et preen-KIH-pih-uum et fohns

to be a writer, you must have something to say

Horace giving us the first step in becoming a writer, literally "knowledge is the foundation and source of good writing." (See also SCRIBIMUS INDOCTI DOCTIQUE POEMATA PASSIM to see what Horace had to say about poets and would-be poets.)

scribere iussit (or **jussit**) amor
SKREE-beh-reh YOOS-seet AH-mawr

you drove me to verse

Ovid explaining why he felt impelled to write, literally "love commanded me to write." He was speaking of writing poetry, not love letters.

scribimus indocti doctique poemata passim
SKREE-bih-muus in-DAWK-tee DAWK-tee-kweh paw-ay-MAH-tah PAHS-sim

everybody wants to get into the act

Horace, vexed with untalented amateur versifiers, sounding off in "learned and unlearned, we all write poems indiscriminately."

scriptorum chorus omnis amat nemus et fugit urbem
skree-PTOH-ruum KAWR-uus AWM-nihs AH-maht NEH-muus et FUU-git UUR-bem

find a place in Vermont to do your best writing

Horace, observing contemporary demographic trends in his day, tells us "the whole band of writers loves the woods and flees the city." Things haven't changed much since then, and today we see much good writing emanating from cabins in the woods.

secundum artem
seh-KUUN-duum AHR-tem
according to the rules of art

secundum ipsius naturam
seh-KUUN-duum ih-PSEE-uus nah-TOO-rahm
according to its very nature

secundum legem
seh-KUUN-duum LAY-gehm
according to law

secundum usum
seh-KUUN-duum OOS-uum
according to custom *or* according to usage

The way we generally use language and conduct ourselves. Or hope to.

secundum veritatem
seh-KUUN-duum way-rih-TAH-tem
universally valid

Literally "according to truth."

se defendendo
say day-fen-DEN-doh
in self-defense

Literally "in defending oneself."

sede vacante
SAY-day wah-KAHN-tay
the seat being vacant

The seat here is the bishop's, called also the see, but *sede vacante* now is also applicable to any position ordinarily designated a seat, for example, a Congressional seat.

sed haec hactenus
sed hīk HAH-kteh-nuus
but so much for this

A good way to close out a topic under discussion in order to turn to another topic. (See also AD MELIORA VERTAMUR.)

seditio civium hostium est occasio
say-DIH-tih-oh KEE-wee-uum HAW-stee-uum est awk-KAH-sih-oh
keep people content and quiet

A lesson in governing, literally "civil discord gives the enemy an opportunity." The enemy may be the political party out of power at home as well as a foreign power with the capacity and inclination to mount a military attack.

semel abbas, semper abbas
SEH-mel AHB-bahs SEM-pehr AHB-bahs
once an abbot, always an abbot

It takes more than an abandonment of ecclesiastical habit or a change of vocation to alter anyone's strongly held beliefs.

semel pro semper
SEH-mel proh SEM-pehr
once for always

semper avarus eget
SEM-pehr ah-WAH-ruus EH-get
avarice is never satisfied

Horace telling us "a greedy man is always in need." (See also DESUNT INOPIAE MULTA, AVARITIAE OMNIA.)

semper et ubique
SEM-pehr et uu-BEE-kweh
always and everywhere

semper felix
SEM-pehr FAY-leeks
always fortunate *or* always successful

semper timidum scelus
SEM-pehr TIH-mih-duum SKEH-luus
crime is always fearful

The guilty live in fear of being found out.

senatus consultum
seh-NAH-tuus kohn-SUUL-tuum
a decree of the senate

The senate of ancient Rome, of course. The U.S. Senate is not empowered to issue decrees. Our courts do that.

senectus insanabilis morbus est
seh-NEK-tuus een-sah-NAH-bih-lihs MAWR-buus est
old age is an incurable disease

But usually considered to be better than dying.

senex bis puer
See BIS PUERI SENES.

sensu bono
SAYN-suu BAW-noh
in a good sense

sensu malo
SAYN-suu MAH-loh
in a bad sense

sequiturque patrem non passibus aequis
seh-kwih-TUUR-kweh PAH-trem nohn PAHS-sih-buus Ī-
kwihs
he's no match for his father

Virgil, speaking of the young son of Aeneas, gave us a
metaphor we can apply to any son of any father, literally "he
follows his father, but not with equal steps." We all know, of
course, that in many father-son combinations the younger
member far outstrips the elder.

sequor non inferior
SEH-kwawr nohn een-FEH-rih-awr
I follow but I am not inferior

Makes for good labor-management relations. Especially in
a democracy.

serus in caelum redeas
SAY-ruus in KĪ-luum REH-deh-ahs
may you live long!

Horace addressed Augustus, his emperor, in these words,
literally "late may you return to heaven," giving us an appropriate toast—but one always to be given in Latin. The literal
English translation does not sit as well as the conventional
toast given above. People usually want to live long, but they
don't want to be reminded that somewhere along the line they
will be going to their so-called great reward.

servabo fidem
sehr-WAH-boh FIH-dem
I will keep the faith

sic eunt fata hominum
seek AY-uunt FAH-tah HAW-mih-nuum
thus go the destinies of men

sic me servavit Apollo
seek may sehr-WAH-wit ah-PAWL-loh
thus Apollo preserved me

Horace, referring to the Greek god of prophecy. Apollo also was the god of a multiplicity of groups and activities.

sic passim
seek PAHS-sim
so here and there throughout

A scholarly phrase intended to direct the reader's attention to the appearance in a text of a particular topic or topics identified by the writer.

sicut meus est mos
SEE-kuut MEH-uus est mohs
as is my habit

sic volo sic iubeo (or jubeo)
seek WAW-loh seek YUU-beh-oh
thus I will, thus I command

Juvenal, giving you a way to make clear that you have every intention of getting your own way.

si fortuna iuvat (or juvat)
see fawr-TOO-nah YUU-waht
if fortune favors

si hic esses, aliter sentires
see heek ES-sehs AH-lih-tehr sen-TEE-rehs
if you were here, you would think otherwise

The rejoinder available when a person who lacks practical knowledge offers advice on how to get out of a difficulty. Consider, for example, the academic theorist instantly ready with a solution for any distressing problem emerging anywhere in the world. Simply say to that person, *Si hic esses, aliter sentires.*

sile et philosophus esto
SIH-lay et fih-LAW-saw-fuus EH-stoh
hold your tongue and you will pass for a philosopher

Literally "be silent and be a philosopher," freely rendered as "be quiet, and people will think you're wise."

silentium altum
sih-LEN-tee-uum AHL-tuum
profound silence

simile simili gaudet
SIH-mih-leh SIH-mih-lih GOW-det
birds of a feather flock together

Literally "like delights in like."

similiter
sih-MIH-lih-tehr
similarly *or* in like manner

simplex munditiis
SIM-pleks muun-DIH-tih-ees
elegant in simplicity

Horace, who knew how to butter people up, used this phrase, literally "natural in (your) elegance," in addressing a beautiful woman.

simpliciter
sim-PLIH-kih-tehr
simply

But also well translated as "naturally," "frankly," "without reserve," and "absolutely."

simul sorbere ac flare non possum
SIH-muul SAWR-beh-reh ahk FLAH-reh nohn PAWS-suum
make up your mind—one way or the other

This homely truth is well translated as "I cannot simultaneously exhale and inhale," more literally as "I cannot swallow and blow at the same time." This expression may be used to tell an ambivalent person to clarify an instruction. It is especially apposite when the driver of a car is told by a pair of backseat drivers to turn both left and right at the next traffic light.

sine anno
SIH-neh AHN-noh
undated

A scholarly notation, literally "without a year," indicating that a cited source carries no reliable date of composition or publication.

sine Cerere et Libero friget Venus
SIH-neh KEH-reh-reh et LEE-beh-roh FREE-get WEH-nuus
love dies on an empty stomach

A realistic adage of Terence that has its charm. Ceres was a goddess of agriculture, Liber a god of wine and vineyards, and Venus a goddess of love. Terence, thus, was telling us literally that "Venus grows cold without Ceres and Liber," more conventionally that "love grows cold without bread and wine."

sine cortice natare
SIH-neh KAWR-tih-keh nah-TAH-reh
to need no assistance

Literally "to swim (or float) without cork."

sine dolo malo
SIH-neh DAW-loh MAH-loh
without deceit

Also translated as "without fraud" and "without evil intent."

sine ictu
SIH-neh IH-ktoo
without a blow *or* without a wound

The amicable way to settle a dispute.

sine ioco (or joco)
SIH-neh YAW-koh
seriously

Literally "without jest."

sine ira et studio
SIH-neh EE-rah et STUU-dee-oh
calmly and fairly

A phrase from Tacitus, literally "without anger and partiality."

sine macula et ruga
SIH-neh MAH-kuu-lah et ROO-gah
without stain or wrinkle

In one's reputation, that is. But also the way we want our clothes to come back from the dry cleaner.

sine nomine vulgus
SIH-neh NOH-mih-neh WUUL-guus
the multitude without a name

An arrogant characterization of ordinary people.

sine pennis volare haud facile est
SIH-neh PEN-nihs waw-LAH-reh howd FAH-kih-leh est
don't try anything you're not ready for

Plautus offering excellent advice, literally "it's not at all easy to fly without wings." Implicit in this statement is encouragement to prepare oneself for new challenges. But consider the legend of Icarus and his father, Daedalus, who were able to flee imprisonment by Minos, king of Crete, on wings built by Daedalus. Unfortunately, Icarus flew so close to the sun that the wax attaching his wings melted and he fell into the Aegean Sea. So we are encouraged by this story not to attempt more than we are able to accomplish.

sine prole superstite
SIH-neh PRO-leh suu-pehr-STIH-teh
without surviving offspring

A legal term.

si peccavi, insciens feci
see pek-KAH-wee EEN-skih-ayns FAY-kee
how to claim innocence when guilty

Terence telling us what to say when we're caught red-handed, literally "If I made a mistake, I did so unwittingly."

si vis ad summum progredi, ab infimo ordiri
see wees ahd SUUM-muum proh-GREH-dee ahb EEN-fih-moh awr-DEE-ree
don't expect too much all at once

Good advice, literally "if you want to reach the top, start at the bottom." Unless your father-in-law owns the business.

si vis amari ama
see wees ah-MAH-ree AH-mah
love is a two-way street

Seneca offering sound advice to the loveless, "if you want to be loved, love." (See also AMOR GIGNIT AMOREM.)

sola nobilitas virtus
SOH-lah noh-BIH-lih-tahs WIHR-tuus
virtue is the only nobility

For an amplified phrase, see NOBILITAS SOLA EST ATQUE UNICA VIRTUS.

spargere voces in vulgum ambiguas
SPAHR-geh-reh WOH-kehs in WUUL-guum ahm-BIH-guu-ahs
how to win elections

Virgil defining the art of propagandizing, literally "to spread equivocal rumor among the multitude."

spectemur agendo
speh-KTEH-muur ah-GEN-doh
let us be judged by our actions

Not by hearsay or how we dress, for example.

spem pretio non emo
spem PREH-tee-oh nohn EH-moh
don't try to sell me expectations

Terence, ever the realist, telling us "I do not pay money for mere hope."

sperate miseri, cavete felices
spay-RAH-teh MIH-seh-ree kah-WAY-tay feh-LEE-kehs
you never know the card you will be dealt next

This maxim, literally "hope, you wretched persons; beware, you successful people," offers valuable advice. Just when life looks bleakest, all may not be lost; just when everything seems to be going your way, you may stumble. For reinforcement of this advice, see also SPERAT INFESTIS, METUIT SECUNDIS.

sperat infestis, metuit secundis
SPAY-raht een-FEHS-tihs MEH-too-iht seh-KUUN-dihs
your present situation is not cast in concrete

Horace, speaking approvingly of the person who does not take the future for granted, tells us literally "he hopes in dangerous times and fears in times of good fortune." (See also SPERATE MISERI, CAVETE FELICES.)

spes sibi quisque
spays SIH-bih KWIHS-kweh
rely on yourself

Virgil telling us not to depend on others, "let each be his own hope."

spicula et faces amoris
SPEE-kuu-lah et FAH-kehs ah-MOH-rihs
love's artillery

If we are to take at face value this phrase, literally "the darts and torches of love," love stings and burns. Fortunately, people seem to be able to withstand such suffering—perhaps for the sake of the children.

splendide mendax
SPLEN-dih-day MEN-dahks
untruthful for good purpose

This brilliant phrase from Horace—one meaning of *splendide* is "brilliantly"—here carries the literal meaning of "nobly untruthful." It is surely applicable to many situations in life, of greater and lesser importance, in which diplomats and spouses, for example, consider a bit of mendacity to be the better part of wisdom. "We accept and will honor an immediate cease-fire."

spretae iniuria (or injuria) formae
SPRAY-tī in-YOO-ree-ah FAWR-mī
the insult of slighted beauty

This phrase from Virgil's *Aeneid* teaches us how much trouble can result from beauty scorned. The story involving beauty scorned began when Paris was chosen to be the judge in the mother of all beauty contests—only three entrants, all of them goddesses: Hera (Juno), Athene (Minerva), and Aphrodite (Venus). Aphrodite promised Paris that if he chose her, she would reward him with the hand of the most beautiful woman in the world. Aphrodite won, of course, and as sure as night follows day, Hera never forgave Paris. This was *spretae iniuria formae*. But the story is not over. Whom did Paris want as his reward from Aphrodite? Helen of Troy. Unfortunately, Helen was already married to the king of Sparta, and when Paris ran off with Helen, there was launched the devastating Trojan War—in which Paris lost his life. So Helen's face may have "launched a thousand ships," in Christopher Marlowe's phrase, but it also "burnt the topless towers of Ilium," again Marlowe's phrase. The moral? It does not pay to slight a vindictive goddess. Especially a beautiful one. (See also TAETERRIMA BELLI CAUSA.)

stant belli causa
stahnt BEL-lee KOW-sah
the causes of war remain

A phrase from Virgil indicating that wars do not settle anything when their outcomes do not repair the unhappy circumstances that led to the wars.

stare decisis, et non quieta movere
STAH-reh day-KEE-sihs et nohn kwee-AY-tah moh-WAY-
reh
to uphold legal precedents

A phrase often abbreviated in our appellate courts as the
principle of "*stare decisis*," in English pronounced STAIR-ee
dih-SĪ-sis, "let the precedent stand." The full Latin phrase may
be translated as "to stand by things decided, and not to disturb
settled issues."

stare super vias antiquas
STAH-reh SUU-pehr WEE-ahs ahn-TEE-kwahs
to cling to the old ways

Literally "to stand upon the ancient ways," also translated
as "to be conservative."

stat fortuna domus virtute
staht fawr-TOO-nah DAW-muus wihr-TOO-teh
everything depends on having a good reputation

Literally "the success of the house stands by its virtue." A
good motto for commercial enterprises that expect to endure
for generations.

stat magni nominis umbra
See NOMINIS UMBRA.

stemmata quid faciunt?
STEM-mah-tah kwid FAH-kee-uunt
you say your family arrived on the Mayflower?

Juvenal giving us what self-made men and the upwardly mobile would consider a splendid rhetorical question, literally "of what value are pedigrees?" But Juvenal did go on to supply a Roman answer. See NOBILITAS SOLA EST ATQUE UNICA VIRTUS.

stilus virum arguit
STIH-luus WIH-ruum AHR-goo-it
the style proves the man

A comment on the uniqueness of rhetorical style. Best known to most of us in the French adage *le style c'est l'homme même*, "the style is the man himself." Count de Buffon, an 18th-century naturalist, spoke these words in his address upon the occasion of his reception into the French Academy.

strenua inertia
STRAY-noo-ah ih-NEHR-tee-ah
energetic idleness

A wonderful oxymoron from Horace, telling us that it often takes a lot of work to appear to keep busy doing nothing. (See also OTIOSA SEDULITAS.)

stricto sensu
STRIK-toh SAYN-soo
in a strict sense

The opposite of LATO SENSU.

studium immane loquendi
STUU-dih-uum ihm-MAH-neh law-KWEN-dee
a prodigious fondness for talking

Ovid's polite term. More often described as **furor** (FUU-rawr) **loquendi**, "a rage for speaking."

stultum facit fortuna quem vult perdere
STUUL-tuum FAH-kit fawr-TOO-nah kwem wuult PEHR-deh-reh
dame fortune first makes a fool out of the man she wishes to destroy

A proverb from Publilius Syrus. Beware, all you wealthy men of advanced age seeking a beautiful wife of twenty-five. Or less.

sua munera mittit cum hamo
SOO-ah MOO-neh-rah MIT-tit kuum HAH-moh
a sprat to catch a whale

This saying, literally "he sends his gifts with a hook attached," suggests a person who makes a concession in the hope of a bigger return. A chess player's gambit is an example of this cunning.

sua si bona norint
SOO-ah see BAW-nah NOH-rint
if they but knew their blessings

A phrase from Virgil. For the full statement see O FORTU-NATOS NIMIUM, SUA SI BONA NORINT!

suave, mari magno turbantibus aequora ventis, e terra magnum alterius spectare laborem
SWAH-way MAH-rih MAH-gnoh tuur-BAHN-tih-buus ī-KWOH-rah WEHN-tihs ay TEHR-rah MAH-gnuum ahl-TAY-rih-uus spek-TAH-reh lah-BOH-rem
it's easy to shout "kill him" from ringside

Sardonic wisdom from Lucretius, literally "it's pleasant when safe on land to watch the great struggle of another out on a swelling sea, amid winds churning the deep."

sublata causa tollitur effectus
suub-LAH-tah KOW-sah TAWL-lih-tuur ef-FEHK-tuus
a real cure

Literally "once the cause is removed, the effect disappears."

sub specie
suub SPEH-kih-ay
under the appearance of *or* under the pretext of

sume superbiam quaesitam meritis
SOO-may suu-PEHR-bih-ahm KWĪ-sih-tahm MEH-rih-tihs
take satisfaction in your accomplishments

Horace telling us literally "assume the pride earned by your good deeds."

summo studio
SUUM-moh STUU-dih-oh
with the greatest zeal

sumptibus publicis
SUUMP-tih-buus POO-blih-kihs
at public expense

Congressional junkets are made *sumptibus publicis.*

sum quod eris, fui quod sis
suum kwawd EH-rihs FUU-ee kwawd sees
I am what you will be, I was what you are

An intentionally chilling Roman tombstone inscription.

sunt bona, sunt quaedam mediocria, sunt mala plura
suunt BAW-nah suunt KWĪ-dahm meh-dih-OH-krih-ah
suunt MAH-lah PLOO-rah
some things are good, some middling, but more are bad

Martial, skewing the normal curve of distribution.

sunt lacrimae rerum
suunt LAH-krih-mī RAY-ruum
human lives are not free of sorrow

Virgil telling us literally "there are tears for things (that have happened)."

suo Marte
SUU-oh MAHR-teh
by one's own exertions

Mars (mahrs) is known especially as the Roman god of war, but he was also the patron of farmers—who work hard and must be prudent managers—and typified divine fortitude.

suo periculo
SUU-oh peh-REE-kuu-loh
at one's own peril

suo sibi gladio hunc iugulo (or jugulo)
SUU-oh SIH-bih GLAH-dih-oh huunk YUU-guu-loh
I'll use this man's own words against him

Terence telling us literally "I will cut this man's throat with his own sword."

superstitione tollenda religio non tollitur
suu-pehr-stih-tih-OH-neh tawl-LEN-dah ray-LIH-gih-oh
nohn TAWL-lih-tuur
religion is not abolished by eliminating superstition

Cicero's observation on the durability of religion. Indeed, the British politician and man of letters Edmund Burke (1729–1797) gave us this aphorism, "Religion, not atheism, is the true remedy for superstition."

suppressio veri, suggestio falsi
suup-PRES-sih-oh WAY-ree suug-GEHS-tih-oh FAHL-sih
suppression of truth is suggestion of falsehood

Press spokespersons, beware.

surgit amari aliquid quod in ipsis floribus angat
SUUR-git ah-MAH-rih AH-lih-kwid kwawd in IH-psihs FLOH-rih-buus AHN-gaht
there's always a fly in the ointment

Lucretius telling us literally "something bitter always arises to poison our sweetest joys."

suspendens omnia naso
suus-PEN-dens AWM-nee-ah NAH-soh
sneering at everything

Horace characterizing a finicky person, literally "turning up the nose at everything."

suspensio per collum
suus-PEN-sih-oh pehr KAWL-luum
a necktie party

Less colloquially, "execution by hanging." Literally, "suspension by the neck."

suspiria de profundis
suus-PEE-rih-ah day praw-FUUN-dees
sighs from the depths

Of the soul, that is.

suum cuique
SOO-uum KWEE-kweh
to each his own

T

tacitae magis et occultae inimicitiae timendae sunt quam indictae atque apertae
TAH-kih-tī MAH-gihs et awk-KUUL-tī ih-nih-mee-KIH-tee-ī tih-MEN-dī suunt kwahm in-DIK-tī AHT-kweh ah-PEHR-tī
it's hard to deal with closet enemies

Cicero, an astute political leader, reflecting on foes he faced, tells us literally that "silent, hidden enmities are more to be feared than those that are openly expressed."

tacitum vivit sub pectore vulnus
TAH-kih-tuum WEE-wit suub PEK-taw-reh WUUL-nuus
a wound unuttered lives deep within the breast

Virgil, centuries before Freud, giving us this helpful insight: it's better not to suffer personal attacks in silence.

taeterrima belli causa
tī-TEHR-rih-mah BEL-lee KOW-sah
the most repulsive cause of war

A powerful characterization by Horace. And what was that cause? Abduction of a woman, Helen of Troy. And how did the ten-year Trojan War turn out? Troy was sacked and burned. (See also SPRETAE INIURIA FORMAE.)

tam Marte quam Minerva
tahm MAHR-teh kwahm mih-NEHR-wah
as much by fighting as by wisdom

Literally "as much by Mars as by Minerva." Mars was the Roman god of war, Minerva the Roman goddess of wisdom. (See also TAM MARTE QUAM MERCURIO.)

tam Marte quam Mercurio
tahm MAHR-teh kwahm mehr-KOO-ree-oh
as much by fighting as by business

Literally "as much by Mars as by Mercury." Mercury was the Roman god of trade. It is interesting to note that, among other hats Mercury wore, he was also the god of thieves. (See also TAM MARTE QUAM MINERVA.)

tamquam in speculum
TAHM-kwahm in SPEH-kuu-luum
as in a mirror

Examine yourself and your motives. (See also VELUTI IN SPECULUM.)

tandem fit surculus arbor
TAHN-dem fit SOOR-kuu-luus AHR-bawr
don't be impatient—they'll grow up

Comfort for parents, literally "a twig at length becomes a tree." (See also PARVIS E GLANDIBUS QUERCUS.)

tantaene animis caelestibus irae?
tahn-TĪ-neh AH-nih-mees kī-LES-tih-buus EE-rī
can heavenly minds yield to such rage?

Virgil remarking on anger shown by the gods.

tantas componere lites
TAHN-tahs kawm-POH-neh-reh LEE-tehs
to settle such great disputes

tantum religio potuit suadere malorum
TAHN-tuum ray-LIH-gee-oh PAW-too-eet soo-ah-DAY-reh mah-LOH-ruum
the effects of religion are not always benign

Homer related that Agamemnon commanded the Greek forces in the invasion of Troy. When Agamemnon's fleet was becalmed en route to Troy, he was willing to offer his daughter Iphigenia as a sacrifice to the goddess Artemis, a huntress. It was this intention that provoked Lucretius to remark *tantum religio potuit suadere malorum,* literally "for how many evils has religion been responsible," more elegantly translated as "such evil deeds could religion prompt." Incidentally, Artemis snatched Iphigenia away before her father could carry out the bloody deed, and when Agamemnon returned from Troy he was himself murdered by his wife Clytemnestra and her lover Aegisthus.

tantus amor scribendi
TAHN-tuus AH-mawr skree-BEN-dee
such a passion for writing

Horace on writers—talented or otherwise—who never give up.

tecum habita, noris quam sit tibi curta supellex
TAY-kuum HAH-bih-tah NOH-rihs kwahm sit TIH-bih KUUR-tah suu-PEL-leks
realize how much you have still to learn

Persius telling us literally "dwell within yourself, you will know how incomplete is your mental furniture."

te hominem esse memento
tay HAW-mih-nem ES-seh meh-MEN-toh
remember you are a man

And nothing more.

tempore felici multi numerantur amici
TEM-paw-reh fay-LEE-kih MUUL-tee nuu-meh-RAHN-
tuur ah-MEE-kee

people flock to the sides of the powerful

Hackneyed but true, literally "we can count many friends
when we are successful." Also given as **felicitas habet mul-
tos amicos** (fay-LEE-kih-tahs HAH-bet MUUL-tohs ah-MEE-
kohs), "prosperity has many friends." (See also UBI AMICI, IBI
OPES.)

tempus omnia revelat
TEM-puus AWM-nee-ah reh-WEL-aht

time reveals everything

tenax et fidelis
TEH-nahks et fih-DAY-lihs

steadfast and faithful

tentanda via est
ten-TAHN-dah WEE-ah est

the way must be tried

Virgil urging us not to give up easily, but to explore any
method that shows promise.

terminus ad quem
TEHR-mih-nuus ahd kwem

a destination

Literally "the end toward which."

terminus ante quem
TEHR-mih-nuus AHN-teh kwem

a point in time before which

More comprehensibly translated as "an established date or time before which an event must have occurred." (See also TERMINUS POST QUEM.)

terminus post quem
TEHR-mih-nuus pawst kwem
a point in time after which

More comprehensibly translated as "an established date or time after which an event must have occurred." (See also TERMINUS ANTE QUEM.)

terrae filius
TEHR-rī FEE-lih-uus
a peasant

Literally "a son of the soil."

terras irradient
TEHR-rahs ihr-RAH-dih-ent
may they illumine the earth

Motto of Amherst College.

tetigisti acu
teh-tih-GIHS-tee AH-koo
you've hit the nail on the head

A phrase from Plautus, literally "you have touched it with a needle." (See also REM ACU TANGERE.)

tibi seris, tibi metis
TIH-bih SEH-rihs TIH-bih MEH-tihs

I am the master of my fate;
I am the captain of my soul.

In these lines from "Invictus," William Ernest Henley tells people that they have individual responsibility for the lives they lead—in the Latin phrase, literally "you sow for yourself, you reap for yourself." (See also UT SEMENTEM FECERIS, ITA METES and AT SPES NON FRACTA.)

time Deum, cole regem
TIH-may DAY-uum KAW-leh RAY-gehm
fear God, honor the king

A worthwhile distinction.

timet pudorem
TIH-met puu-DOH-rem
he (or she) fears shame

Also translated as "he (or she) fears disgrace."

timidi mater non flet
TIH-mih-dee MAH-tehr nohn flet
think of your mother and don't take undue risks

Probably intended sardonically, since this advice, literally "the mother of a timid man does not weep," is not what we would expect from Romans.

timor belli
TIH-mawr BEL-lee
fear of war

timor fecit deos
TIH-mawr FAY-kit DAY-ohs
fear, all-powerful fear

When faced with awesome and unexplainable natural phenomena, the ancients sought supernatural explanations, giving us this phrase, literally "fear created the gods." And throughout time, many soldiers in the grip of fear have been known to call on God to protect them. (See also IN VOTA MISEROS ULTIMUS COGIT TIMOR.)

timor mortis morte peior
TIH-mawr MAWR-tihs MAWR-teh PAY-awr
fear of death is worse than death

Perhaps.

toto caelo errare
TOH-toh KĪ-loh ehr-RAH-reh
to be greatly mistaken

Literally "to err by the entire heaven." Talk about being off the mark!

trahimur omnes studio laudis, et optimus quisque maxime gloria ducitur
TRAH-hih-muur AWM-nehs STUU-dih-oh LOW-dihs et AW-ptih-muus KWIHS-kweh MAH-ksih-may GLOH-ree-ah DOO-kih-tuur
how we are misled by our yearning for fame

Cicero speaking to all of us past and present who have exhibited an inordinate desire to achieve fame, literally "we are all impelled by a desire to be praised, and the higher a man's standing, the more he is deceived by glory."

trahit sua quemque voluptas
TRAH-hit SOO-ah KWEM-kweh waw-LUU-ptahs
we all have our own quirks

Virgil reminding us literally that "his own pleasure draws each man."

tristis eris si solus eris
TRIH-stihs EH-rihs see SOH-luus EH-rihs
you will be sad if you remain alone

Ovid encouraging us to take a mate—or at least a close friend.

truditur dies die
TROO-dih-tuur DEE-ays DEE-ay
days on end

Horace commenting on the tedium of life, literally "a day is pushed onward by a day," better translated as "one day follows on the heels of another."

tu enim, Caesar, civitatem dare potes hominibus, verba non potes

See CAESAR NON SUPRA GRAMMATICOS.

U

ubi amici, ibi opes
OO-bee ah-MEE-kee IH-bih AW-pays
where there are friends, there is wealth

Suggesting unfortunately, that too many people seek out the company of wealthy men.

ubi ius (or jus), ibi officium
OO-bee yoos IH-bih awf-FIH-kih-uum
privilege does not come free

Literally "where there is a right, there is also a duty."

ubi ius (or jus), ibi remedium
OO-bee yoos IH-bih reh-MEH-dih-uum
where law prevails, there is a remedy

For every injustice, that is.

ubi ius (or jus) incertum, ibi ius (or jus) nullum
OO-bee yoos in-KEHR-tuum IH-bih yoos NUUL-luum
uncertainty destroys law

Literally "where the law is uncertain, there is no law." When carried to an extreme, the result is anarchy—essentially no law.

ubi panis, ibi patria
OO-bee PAH-nihs IH-bih PAH-trih-ah
above all, I must eat

The motto, literally "wherever there is bread, there is my country," of people in desperate economic circumstances who are intent on fleeing their homeland to seek a better life.

ultimus Romanorum
UUL-tih-muus roh-mah-NOH-ruum
the last of the Romans

This title pays tribute to personal character and achievement as well as implying recognition of the contributions ancient Rome made to Western civilization. "The last of the Romans" has been attached to a number of historical and literary personages, including Brutus (Marcus Junius Brutus)—the famed Roman senator and leader in the assassination of Julius Caesar—William Congreve, Samuel Johnson, and Horace Walpole. The title, whether in Latin or in English, has fallen into disuse in recent times.

ultra posse nemo obligatur
UUL-trah PAWS-seh NAY-moh aw-blih-GAH-tuur
don't bite off more than you can chew

Good advice, literally "no one is obliged to do more than he (or she) can."

una et eadem persona
OO-nah et ay-AH-dem pehr-SOH-nah
one and the same person

uni aequus virtuti, atque eius amicis
OO-nee Ī-kwuus wihr-TOO-tih AHT-kweh AY-uus ah-MEE-kees

friendly to virtue alone and to its friends

A phrase from Horace suggesting that virtue is the motivator underlying the activities and beliefs of good people. Nothing else counts for as much.

unica virtus necessaria
OO-nih-kah WIHR-tuus neh-kehs-SAH-rih-ah

virtue is the only thing necessary

uni navi ne committas omnia
OO-nih NAH-wih nay kawm-MIT-tahs AWM-nee-ah

don't put all your eggs in one basket

A Roman metaphor, literally "don't commit everything (you own) to one ship," advising us to act prudently in any project we undertake—especially when investing for retirement income.

unius dementia dementes efficit multos
OO-nee-uus day-MEN-tih-ah day-MEN-tehs ef-FIH-kit MUUL-tohs

insanity is catching

Literally "the madness of one person drives many mad." Particularly when that person holds a position of leadership.

uno animo
OO-noh AH-nih-moh

unanimously

Literally "with *or* of one mind."

uno ictu
OO-noh IH-ktoo
at a single blow

uno saltu
OO-noh SAHL-too
at a single leap

unum post aliud
OO-nuum pawst AH-lee-uud
one thing at a time

Literally "one thing after another."

urbem latericiam invenit, marmoream reliquit
UUR-bem lah-teh-RIH-kih-ahm in-WAY-nit mahr-MAWR-
ay-ahm reh-LEE-kweet
he found the city brick and left it marble

With these words Suetonius was praising Caesar Augustus
(63 B.C.–A.D. 14), the first Roman emperor. Augustus was noted
for his patronage of the arts, and in his reign Latin literature
flourished. Indeed, the Augustan Age is considered the golden
age of Latin literature.

usque ad satietatem
UUS-kweh ahd sah-tih-eh-TAH-tem
even to the point of satiety

This is how to describe your condition when you've had
more than enough—of anything.

usus est optimus magister
OO-suus est AW-ptih-muus MAH-gih-stehr
experience is the best teacher

See also EXPERIENTIA DOCET and USUS TE PLURA DOCEBIT.

usus est tyrannus
OO-suus est tih-RAHN-nuus
custom is a tyrant

usus te plura docebit
OO-suus tay PLOO-rah DAW-keh-bit
experience will teach you many things

See also EXPERIENTIA DOCET and USUS EST OPTIMUS MAGISTER.

ut ameris, amabilis esto
uut ah-MEH-rihs ah-MAH-bih-lihs EH-stoh
how can you be loved if you are not lovable?

Ovid giving sound advice, literally "that you may be loved, be lovable." (See also AMOR GIGNIT AMOREM and SI VIS AMARI AMA.)

ut homo est, ita morem geras
uut HAW-moh est IH-tah MOH-rem GEH-rahs
a prescription for tolerance

Terence giving us good advice for getting along with other people, literally "as a man is, so must you humor him." Also translated as "suit the manner to the man."

utinam noster esset
UU-tih-nahm NAW-stehr ES-set
we want him on our side

Literally "would that he were ours."

ut pignus amicitiae
uut PIH-gnuus ah-mee-KIH-tih-ī
as a token of friendship

ut sementem feceris, ita metes
uut say-MEN-tem FAY-keh-rihs IH-tah MEH-tehs
as you sow, so shall you reap

See also TIBI SERIS, TIBI METIS.

ut tamquam scopulum sic fugias insolens verbum
uut TAHM-kwahm SKAW-puu-luum seek FUU-gih-ahs
EEN-saw-layns WEHR-buum
avoid the unusual word as if it were a cliff

Advice to orators from Caesar, and good advice it is for
those who want to be understood and convince others.

V

vectigalia nervi sunt rei publicae
wek-tee-GAH-lee-ah NEHR-wee suunt REH-ee POO-
blih-kī
taxes are the sinews of the state

The words of Cicero, who knew how much war and other
state activities cost. Today's politicians are not always bold
enough to say this. (See also NERVI BELLI, PECUNIA INFINITA.)

vel prece vel pretio
wel PREH-keh wel PREH-tee-oh
for love or money

Literally "either by entreaty or by bribe." (See also NEC PRECE
NEC PRETIO.)

veluti in speculum
WEH-luu-tee in SPEH-kuu-luum
you're one too

This rejoinder, literally "just as if in a mirror," is appropriate when reference is made to one's own faults. (See also TAMQUAM IN SPECULUM.)

venalis populus, venalis curia patrum
way-NAH-lihs PAW-puu-lihs way-NAH-lihs KOO-ree-ah PAH-truum
every man has his price

Literally "the people are venal, and the senate is equally venal." This was said of the Roman Senate, and today some believe that nothing much has changed over the centuries.

vendidit hic auro patriam
WAYN-dih-dit heek OW-roh PAH-trih-ahm
this man sold his country for gold

Virgil excoriating a traitor.

veniam pro laudo peto
WEH-nih-ahm proh LOW-doh PEH-toh
just give me a chance to be heard

Ovid addressing his critics, literally "I seek indulgence rather than praise."

venia necessitati datur
WEH-nih-ah neh-kehs-sih-TAH-tih DAH-tuur
we show kindness to those who are truly in need

Literally "indulgence is granted to necessity." Or so we like to think. (See also NECESSITAS NON HABET LEGEM.)

venienti occurrite morbo
weh-nee-EN-tih awk-KUUR-rih-teh MAWR-boh
an ounce of prevention is worth a pound of cure

Persius encouraging preventive medicine with the literal injunction: "forestall oncoming disease." But what Persius told us can apply to other threats to our well-being as well as to life and limb.

venit summa dies et ineluctabile tempus
WEH-nit SUUM-mah DEE-ays et in-ay-luu-KTAH-bih-leh TEM-puus
here comes big trouble for the Dow Jones Average

Virgil, seeing that the fall of Troy was imminent, has given prophets of doom the right words to use in sounding the death knell, literally "the final day has come and the inescapable moment."

venter non habet aures
WEN-tehr nohn HAH-bet OW-rays
don't preach to a starving family

Literally "the belly has no ears." It takes more than words to satisfy hungry people.

ventis secundis
WEN-tees seh-KUUN-dees
when things are going your way

Literally "with favorable winds."

vera incessu patuit dea
WAY-rah in-KES-soo PAH-too-it DAY-ah

> She walks in beauty, like the night
> Of cloudless climes and starry skies

While not matching Lord Byron in metaphoric grandeur, Virgil tells us "she walked with the dignity of a goddess," literally "by her gait the true goddess was revealed."

verbera, sed audi
WEHR-beh-rah sed OW-dee
don't shoot the messenger

Literally "beat me, but hear me out."

vere scire est per causas scire
WAY-ray SKEE-reh est pehr KOW-sahs SKEE-reh
you have to get to the bottom of things

Literally "to know truly is to know causes," more freely "real knowledge lies in understanding causes."

veritas nihil veretur nisi abscondi
WAY-rih-tahs NIH-hil WEH-reh-tuur NIH-sih ahb-SKAWN-dih
truth fears nothing but concealment

See also OBSCURIS VERA INVOLVENS.

veritas praevalebit
WAY-rih-tahs prī-WAH-leh-bit
truth will prevail

Usually.

veritas temporis filia
WAY-rih-tahs TEM-paw-rihs FEE-lee-ah
the truth will out

It just takes a bit of time, literally "truth is the daughter of time." (See also VERITATEM DIES APERIT.)

veritatem dies aperit
way-rih-TAH-tem DEE-ays ah-PEH-rit
time reveals the truth

See also VERITAS TEMPORIS FILIA.

ver perpetuum
wayr pehr-PEH-tuu-uum
perpetual spring

> We can always look forward to a fresh start.

vestigia morientis libertatis
weh-STEE-gee-ah maw-rih-EN-tihs lee-behr-TAH-tihs
the footprints of expiring liberty

> We ignore such signs at great peril to society.

vestis virum facit
WEH-stihs WIH-ruum FAH-kit
clothes make the man

veteris vestigia flammae
WEH-teh-rihs weh-STEE-gee-ah FLAHM-mī
remnants of an ancient flame

> Virgil commenting on Dido's passion for Aeneas. Dido was the queen of Carthage who fell in love with Aeneas when he was shipwrecked and committed herself to the flames after he left Carthage. Talk about old flames! This was the original.

vexata quaestio
weh-KSAH-tah KWĪ-stih-oh
a vexing or distressing question

> Also given as QUAESTIO VEXATA.

victrix fortunae sapientia
WIH-ktreeks fawr-TOO-nī sah-pih-EN-tih-ah
wisdom is the winner over good luck

> Juvenal had this right, at least in the long run.

vide et crede
WIH-day et KRAY-day
see and believe

> We are being told to believe our eyes.

videtur
WIH-day-tuur
it appears *or* it seems

vigilantibus, non dormientibus, iura (or jura) subveniunt
wih-gih-LAHN-tih-buus nohn dawr-mih-EN-tih-buus
YOO-rah suub-WEH-nih-uunt
laws help the watchful, not the sleeping

> So be alert to what laws allow—and do not allow. Otherwise, you will not know what your rights and restrictions are.

vile donum, vilis gratia
WEE-leh DOH-nuum WEE-lihs GRAH-tee-ah
poor gift, poor thanks

> It's not the thought that counts? Better shop at Tiffany's.

vilius argentum est auro, virtutibus aurum
WEE-lee-uus ahr-GEN-tuum est OW-roh wihr-TOO-tih-buus OW-ruum
money isn't everything

> Horace telling us literally "silver is of less value than gold, gold less than virtue."

vincere aut mori
WIN-keh-reh owt MAW-ree
to conquer or die

vino tortus et ira
WEE-noh TAWR-tuus et EE-rah
racked by wine and anger

Horace's characterization of a pugnacious drunk.

vino vendibili hedera non opus est
WEE-noh wayn-DIH-bih-lih HEH-deh-rah nohn AW-puus est
word of mouth may be all you need

Literally "a popular wine needs no ivy." Ivy was sacred to Bacchus, a Greek god of wine, so the ivy bush was displayed on signs outside Roman taverns. To demonstrate that old ways do not die easily, an English proverb dating back to the 16th century has it that "good wine needs no bush."

vires acquirit eundo
WEE-rays ahk-KWEE-rit ay-UUN-doh
once a story finds its legs, it's hard to stop

Virgil, speaking of rumor or gossip, tells us literally "it gains strength as it goes." (See also FAMA NIHIL EST CELERIUS.)

virescit vulnere virtus
wih-RAY-skit WUUL-neh-reh WIHR-tuus
courage flourishes from a wound

And that's why even severely wounded soldiers have been known to continue to fight, performing acts of heroism well above and beyond the call of duty.

virtus ariete fortior
WIHR-tuus ah-ree-EH-tay FAWR-tih-awr
virtue is stronger than a battering ram

Virtus, "virtue," here may also be interpreted as "valor" or as "heroism."

virtus in actione consistit
WIHR-tuus in ahk-tee-OH-neh kohn-SIH-stit
valor lies in action

> Not in words.

virtus incendit vires
WIHR-tuus in-KEN-dit WEE-rays
manhood rouses one's strength

virtus vincit invidiam
WIHR-tuus WIN-kit in-WIH-dih-ahm
virtue overcomes envy

virtute et fide
wihr-TOO-teh et FIH-day
by virtue and faith

virtute non astutia
wihr-TOO-teh nohn ah-STOO-tih-ah
by excellence, not by cunning

virtute non verbis
wihr-TOO-teh nohn WEHR-bees
by virtue, not by words

virtuti non armis fido
wihr-TOO-tih nohn AHR-mihs FEE-doh
I trust to virtue, not to arms

virum volitare per ora
WIH-ruum waw-lih-TAH-reh pehr OH-rah
to spread like wildfire

> Literally "to fly through the mouths of men." The allusion is
to gossip, rumor, and news.

vis a fronte
wees ah FRAWN-teh
a propelling force from in front

vis a tergo
wees ah TEHR-goh
a propelling force from behind

vis comica
wees KOH-mih-kah
comic power *or* comic talent

vis conservatrix naturae
wees kohn-sehr-WAH-treeks nah-TOO-rī
the preserving power of nature

> See also VIS MEDICATRIX NATURAE.

vis inertiae
wees ih-NEHR-tih-ī
passive resistance to force applied

> Literally "the power of idleness."

vis maior (or major)
wees MAH-yawr
greater force *or* superior force

> A legal term denoting circumstances beyond one's control.

vis medicatrix naturae
wees meh-dih-KAH-treeks nah-TOO-rī
the healing power of nature

> See also VIS CONSERVATRIX NATURAE.

vitae praecepta beatae
WEE-tī prī-KAY-ptah beh-AH-tī
directions for a happy life

vitiis nemo sine nascitur
WIH-tih-ees NAY-moh SIH-neh NAH-skee-tuur
no one is born without faults

> A truth from Horace. (See also ABUNDANT DULCIBUS VITIIS.)

vive memor leti
WEE-way MEH-mawr LAY-tee
live as though today were your last

> Persius telling us soberly and literally "live mindful of death."

vivimus in posteris
WEE-wih-muus in PAW-steh-rihs
we live in our posterity

> And that's why we must do everything we can to nurture our children and grandchildren. (See also CULPAM MAIORUM POSTERI LUUNT.)

vivit post funera virtus
WEE-wit pawst FOO-neh-rah WIHR-tuus
your good deeds won't be forgotten

> Literally "excellence survives the grave."

volat hora per orbem
WAW-laht HOH-rah pehr AWR-bem
time flies

> Literally "time flies through the world." Also given as **tempus fugit** (TEM-puus FUU giht) "time flies."

voluptates corporis
waw-luu-PTAH-tehs KAWR-paw-rihs
sensual pleasures

> Literally "the pleasures of the body."

volventibus annis
wawl-WEN-tih-buus AHN-nihs
as time goes by

> Virgil observing the passage of time, literally "with the years rolling on."

vox faucibus haesit
wawks FOW-kih-buus HĪ-sit
he was struck dumb

> Virgil giving us his version of how it feels to find yourself speechless with amazement, literally "the voice stuck in the throat."

vox stellarum
wawks stayl-LAH-ruum
the music of the spheres

> Literally "the voice of the stars."

vulgus ignobile
WUUL-guus ih-GNOH-bih-leh
the low-born rabble

vulnus immedicabile
WUUL-nuus im-meh-dih-KAH-bih-leh
an incurable wound

English Index

a man of no political party, 128
a man of three letters, 128
an act done against my will is not
    my act, 11
an act of God injures nobody, 11
and also, 9
and elsewhere, 100
and even, 9
and may it be lucky, prosperous,
    and auspicious!, 211
and other men, 101
and other things, 101
and other women, 101
anew, 4
an angry lover tells himself many
    lies, 29
an independent man, 128
another's faults are before our eyes,
    our own are behind us, 24
another's money, 21
another thing and yet the same, 27
another way must be tried, 24
not the antidote before the poison,
    170
about anything worthless, 88
any way you slice it, it's still plagia-
    rism, 147
thus Apollo preserved me, 230
the apparatus of war, 36
an appeal based on the possibility of
    profit, 12
everyone is the architect of his own
    failure, 110
an argument for harsh justice, 210
by armed force, 153
arms are the props of peace, 38
arms guard peace, 39
a royal grant, 214
as far as I know, 212
ashes to ashes and dust to dust, 85
as if he had said, 206
as if said, 206
as is my habit, 230
as the king, so the flock, 205
ask not for whom the bell tolls, 163
ask for what is unreasonable so that
    you may obtain what is just,
    136
as long as he behaves well, 205

as long as the money holds out,
    175
as long as a sick man has breath, he
    has hope, 20
as a man is, so you must humor him,
    255
as matters stand, 99
as in a mirror, 245
as much by fighting as by business,
    245
as much by fighting as by wisdom,
    244
as much by Mars as by Mercury,
    245
as much by Mars as by Minerva,
    245
as nearly as possible, 206
a son of the people, 116
an ass at the lyre, 39
an ass is beautiful to an ass, and a
    pig to a pig, 39
as soon as possible, 205
assume the pride earned by your
    good deeds, 241
assuredly a goddess, 84
as things are, 99
as time goes by, 266
as you sow, so shall you reap, 3,
    256
at all hours, 169
at the beginning, 15
at the crossroads, 12
at a favorable moment, 90
at hand, 16
at last, 12
at my own risk, 157
atoms, 217
at one's convenience, 105
at one's own peril, 242
at our own risk, 178
at a place where two ways meet, 12
at public expense, 241
at a single blow, 254
attached to the soil, 18
he attains whatever he attempts, 70
at this time, 126
audacity serves as a defense, 40
an auspicious omen, 183
avarice is never satisfied, 228

common consent, 68
common danger creates unity, 68
common opinion, 68
a companion on the road is as good
   as a carriage, 67
to compare great things with small,
   191
to compare small things with great,
   191
comparisons are odious, 105
in complete cooperation, 70
compliance breeds friends, truth
   hatred, 181
without compromising one's dignity,
   221
the conditions agreed upon, 188
confessedly, 105
confusedly, 2
in confusion, 165
to conquer or die, 261
either to conquer or to die, 43
with conscience intact, 221
conscience is worth a thousand witnesses, 70
the conscript fathers, 191
contemplate, 25
it is contrary to nature, 185
control your temper, 68
conveniently, 105
cop a plea, 126
corruption of the best is worst, 75
could you help laughing, my
   friends?, 219
count your blessings, 182
by courage and faith, 33
by courage, not by cunning, 34
courage flourishes from a wound,
   262
covetous, 25
covetous for another's property,
   wasteful of his own, 25
a cowardly dog barks more than it
   bites, 56
the cowl does not make the monk,
   79
crazy in love, 29
a credulous thing is love, 77
the crime of falsehood, 78
the crime of forgery, 78

crime is always fearful, 228
crime levels those whom it contaminates, 111
a criminal is a criminal is a criminal,
   111
cross, 78
cupboard love, 182
currying favor, 57
the custom of the place is to be
   observed, 71
custom is the best interpreter of
   laws, 71
custom is observed as law, 72
custom is a tyrant, 255
to cut the throats of the dead, 140

D

dame fortune first makes a fool out
   of the man she wishes to
   destroy, 240
danger comes sooner when it is not
   feared, 65
the dangers of great success, 149
dare to be wise, 41
dare to think independently, 41
in darkness, 138
the darts and torches of love, 236
dawn, 35
a day is pushed onward by a day,
   251
days on end, 251
a deadly war, 45
dead men don't sue, 9
dead tired, you'll sleep anywhere,
   113
death, 85
death before dishonor, 152
either death or victory, 42
death is common to all, 159
death is the final boundary of things,
   159
death is the final reckoning, 159
death is the gate of life, 159
death levels all things, 184
debt, 21
the debt to nature, 85
to deceive magnificently, 156
a decree of the senate, 228
deeds, 217

a great fortune is a great slavery, 149

great is the power of conscience, 150

great is the power of habit, 149

great things have small beginnings, 191

greed, greed, greed, 208

greedy for another's property, 25

a greedy man is always in need, 228

Greek, 208

gross neglect, 80

gross negligence, 76

above all, guard your credit rating, 115

the guardian of morals, 63

guard your reputation as your life, 50

to be guilty of solecisms, 92

H

habit is, as it were, second nature, 72

a hand from the clouds, 153

by the hands of many a great load is lightened, 161

handsome is as handsome does, 223

happy are they who have kept a middle course, 155

happy the man who lives far away from the cares of business, 45

hard work commands respect, 157

even hares insult a dead lion, 159

haste is late, 115

to have spread wings greater than the nest, 150

having gotten one's wish, 69

having well deserved, 47

the hazard of war is uncertain, 23

the healing power of nature, 264

hear no evil, see no evil, speak no evil, 42

hearsay, 84

a hearsay report, 91

hear, see, be silent if you wish to live in peace, 42

heart speaks to heart, 73

heaven at last!, 89

he brooks no equal, 190

he conquers twice who conquers

himself in the hour of victory, 50

he died without issue, 85

he fears shame, 249

he follows his father, but not with equal steps, 229

he has died well, 46

he has gone, he has made off, he has escaped, he has broken away, 4

he has gone to the ancestors, 3

he has it, 126

he has not lived ill who has been born and died unnoticed, 168

he hopes in dangerous times and fears in times of good fortune, 236

he is absent, 2

he is alarmed before the trumpet sounds, 35

he is deserving who is industrious, 157

he is hit, 126

he is no writer whose verses no one reads, 177

he is scared stiff, 74

he labors in vain who strives to please everybody, 118

help after the war, 198

help from on high, 44

he merits praise who does what he ought to do, not what he is allowed to do, 130

he often quarrels about goat's wool, 219

he owes nothing, 171

he quarrels about nothing, 219

in herds, 122

here comes big trouble for the Dow Jones Average, 258

here lies the hare, 125

here's the problem, 125

heroism, 262

her sparkling eyes bedewed with tears, 142

he sends his gifts with a hook attached, 240

he's flown the coop, 3

he's had it, 126

to live by desperate means, 96
to live evilly is a kind of death, 120
to live from hand to mouth, 135
live as though today were your last, 265
a load cheerfully borne becomes light, 144
lofty towers fall with a greater crash, 62
loneliness, 148
long life!, 17
long time no see, 124
a loss that is unknown is no loss at all, 32
lovable folly, 29
lovable madness, 29
love begets love, 32
love commanded me to write, 225
love and a cough cannot be hidden, 32
love dies on an empty stomach, 232
love grows cold without bread and wine, 233
love is blind, 169
love is a kind of military service, 158
love is a two-way street, 235
to love and be wise is scarcely granted even to a god, 30
the love of money grows as wealth increases, 77
love of possessing, 32
lovers are lunatics, 185
love's artillery, 236
love as warfare, 158
the low-born rabble, 266
loyalty gained through bribes is lost through bribes, 200
loyalty isn't for sale, 199
a lucky break, 153
at a lucky moment, 90

M

madness, 29
madness from drinking, 153
the madness of one person drives many mad, 253
to make a mistake twice in a war is not allowable, 49

to make Priscian's head smaller, 92
you can't make a silk purse out of a sow's ear, 175
make me aware, 112
make up your mind—one way or the other, 232
make your move, 110
you're making an elephant out of a fly, 97
manhood rejoices in trial, 119
manhood rouses one's strength, 263
man is to man either a god or a wolf, 127
man of letters, 127
a man forced to obey is not at fault for what he does, 96
that man got the cross as the reward for crime, this man a crown, 131
a man of his own law, 128
a man of much learning, 127
a man of no color, 128
a man of the old-time virtue and good faith, 35
a man of proven ability, 130
a man who is suddenly generous pleases fools, but his tricks make no impression on the experienced, 216
a man whose opinions are unknown, 128
a man's house is his castle, 93
many grains make a heap, 106
many hands make light work, 161
many things are wanting, 89
many a true word is said in jest, 219
marginal notes, 154
marriageable years, 34
massacre, 15
master of ceremonies, 148
master of the feast, 218
master the material and the words will follow, 216
the material facts, 217
the matrimonial halter, 57
matter is indestructible, 136
the matter being unfinished, 215
a matter of chance, 60
matters unknown, 218
of mature judgment, 98

what is true and seemly, 209

what once were vices now are customs, 204

what one would least suppose, 212

what prohibits one from speaking the truth even while laughing?, 219

what suffices is enough, 223

what to do when someone won't listen, 98

and what had been only a footpath became a highway, 102

what a woman says to an ardent lover should be written on wind and running water, 160

what you don't know won't hurt you, 32

when families fall apart, 8

when the going gets tough, the tough get going, 108

when the money dries up, the game is over, 170

when money talks, everybody listens, 94

when one dog barks, another dog immediately barks, 143

when in Rome, do as the Romans do, 71

when someone starts giving money away, look out, 216

when things are going your way, 258

when things get iffy, you find out who your true friends are, 31

when a tree falls unheard in a forest, 177

when the tree is felled, anyone gathers the wood, 88

when the winds fail, take to the oars, 89

when a woman thinks alone she is plotting mischief, 160

when your neighbor's house is on fire, you are in danger yourself, 163

when you wish to dignify a bad thing, condemn it, 151

where duty and glory lead, 213

where the law is uncertain, there is no law, 252

where law prevails, there is a duty, 251

where law prevails, there is a remedy, 251

where peace and glory lead, 213

where there are friends, there is wealth, 251

where there is a right, there is also a duty, 251

where there's life, there's hope, 19

where there's smoke, there's fire, 116

where were you when I needed you?, 198

whichever of two parties makes the division, the other makes the choice, 79

which is to be especially noted, 211

which thing is absurd, 211

that which Jove is permitted, an ox is not, 212

while drinking, 137

while I breathe, I hope, 180

while there's life there's hope, 180

whither the Fates call, 213

to all who see this document, 184

who cares what people say?, 197

who does not know the rest?, 63

whoever spares the wicked harms the good, 51

who guesses best is the best prophet, 48

who has lived in obscurity, 48

whom Jupiter wishes to destroy, he first makes mad, 206

who spares the guilty punishes the innocent, 211

he who envies is the less for it, 210

he who is free to sin sins less, 79

he who proves too much proves nothing, 210

he who takes a disparaging remark on himself has done it, 207

why are you laughing?, 208

why a blind person with a mirror?, 207